AIRFRAME & POWERPLANT MECHANICS

AIRFRAME WORKBOOK
Written, Oral, and Practical

ALIGNS WITH
FAA-H-8083-31B & FAA-H-8083-31B-ATB
Airframe & Powerplant Mechanics Airframe Handbook

by Ronald Sterkenburg

Aircraft Technical Book Company
72413 US Hwy 40 - Tabernash, CO 80478-0270 USA
(970) 726-5111
www.actechbooks.com

Copyright 2023 - Aircraft Technical Book Company. All rights reserved. Except as permitted under the United States Copyright Act of 1976, no part of this publication may be reproduced or distributed in any form or by any means, or stored in a database retrieval system, without the prior written permission of the publisher.

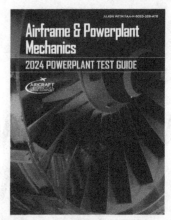

Test Guides For Your 8083 Handbooks
Your Source For All FAA Exam Questions

Just like this Workbook, ATB Test Guides are designed around the FAA Handbooks. Every sample question is derived directly from the 8083's and match the content you will be tested on during your FAA exams.
No other Test Guide can make these claims!

ATB Test Guides Include
- Sample questions, answers, and explanations, all with page references to the handbooks.
- Oral and Practical questions and sample projects for each Handbook chapter.
- A clutter free layout with answers placed out of sight on the backside of each page.
- The complete Airman's Certification Standards (ACS) with each section.
- Available in paper or PDF eBook.

Skyprep Interactive Test Guides
A Digital Solution That's Mobile

Rather than, or in addition to your Test Guide book, Skyprep puts you behind the screen like an actual FAA exam. Choose sample questions randomly, by topic or as an actual timed exam. Your sessions are graded along with answers and explanations for wrong choices. With Skyprep, find out exactly where you stand and where you need more work.

ATB Test Guides and SkyPrep — Your Key To Success With Your FAA Exams!
For more information visit: www.actechbooks.com/ap-testaides.html or
Call (970) 726-5111 - Order both together and save!

PREFACE

This Student Workbook is designed as a companion to the Aviation Maintenance Mechanics Airframe Handbooks FAA-H-8083-31 and FAA-H-8083-31B-ATB. Each chapter of this workbook matches the equivalent chapter in the Handbook and contains study questions, exercises, and a final exam for that chapter. Each is designed to enhance your understanding of the material in the textbook and to better prepare you for success with your actual FAA written exams and later in your career as a professional aviation maintenance technician.

Each chapter of this Workbook is presented in 3 parts:
1. Study Aid Questions are fill in the blank, multiple choice, true or false, or matching formats designed to reinforce the most important concepts presented in the Handbook.
2. Knowledge Application Questions; giving you an opportunity to actually use the material presented in each chapter to solve common problems.
3. Final Chapter Exam, in multiple choice format designed to further reinforce your study skills and to be used by instructors as end of chapter exam and as an evaluation of your progress.

The answers to Sections A and B questions may be found in the back of this workbook and can so be used by students as a part of your personal study habits. The answers to Section C - Final Chapter Exams, are available only to instructors as part of the instructor support package for the H-8083 textbook series, thus preserving the value of the exam as a valid instructional tool.

Each page in this book is perforated allowing students to tear out and turn in assigned sections which may be given as homework or in-class exercises.

For further information about this Workbook, its corresponding Textbook, or to order additional copies in print or electronic format, please contact Aircraft Technical Book Company at 970.726.5111, or email to *orders@actechbooks.com*, or visit our web site at *www.actechbooks.com*.

TABLE OF CONTENTS

Chapter 1	Aircraft Structures	1
Chapter 2	Aerodynamics, Assembly and Rigging	9
Chapter 3	Aircraft Fabric Covering	19
Chapter 4	Aircraft Metal Structural Repair	29
Chapter 5	Aircraft Welding	41
Chapter 6	Aircraft Wood and Structural Repair	53
Chapter 7	Advanced Composite Materials	61
Chapter 8	Aircraft Painting and Finishing	73
Chapter 9	Aircraft Electrical System	81
Chapter 10	Aircraft Instrument Systems	97
Chapter 11	Communication and Navigation	109
Chapter 12	Hydraulic and Pneumatic Power Systems	121
Chapter 13	Aircraft Landing Gear Systems	135
Chapter 14	Aircraft Fuel System	147
Chapter 15	Ice and Rain Protection	159
Chapter 16	Cabin Environmental Control Systems	171
Chapter 17	Fire Protection Systems	183
Answers	Section A and B Answers	193

PAGE LEFT BLANK INTENTIONALLY

AIRCRAFT STRUCTURES

CHAPTER 1

Section A
Study Aid Questions - Fill In The Blanks

1. The part of the aircraft that is designed to carry a load or resist stress is the _____.

2. All aircraft are subjected to five major stresses: tension, compression, bending, _____, and _____.

3. Tensile strength is measured in _____ which is written as _____.

4. Wings that require no external bracing are known as _____ design.

5. _____ internal structures are made up of spars and stringers.

6. Spars are to wings as _____ are to the fuselage.

7. I-beam spars are made up of two components: the _____ which is the vertical section and the _____ which is the horizontal section.

8. 8A stainless steel or titanium bulkhead known as a _____ is used to isolate the _____ from the rest of the aircraft.

9. Cowl flaps are movable parts of the cowling that open and close to _____.

10. The primary flight controls include the ailerons, elevators, and rudders which control the stability around the _____, _____, and _____ axes respectively.

11. Primary flight control surfaces need to be balanced so they do not vibrate or _____.

12. When the aircraft is turned to the left, the aileron on the pilot's _____ points up.

13. Elevators move the aircraft around the _____ axis.

14. When the right pedal is pushed forward, it deflects the rudder to the _____ which moves the nose of the aircraft to the right.

15. Flaps that slide aft to increase the total area of the wing are known as _____ flaps.

16. Slats increase the _____ at which laminar airflow can exist.

17. Heavy or high performance aircraft have _____ on the top of their wings that disrupt airflow when deployed.

AIRCRAFT STRUCTURES

18. The _____ is the location from which all other stations are located.

19. Firewalls are typically made from _____.

20. Teetering hinges in a semi-rigid system allow for movement of the flap _____ while preventing movement _____.

Section A
True of False

_____ 1. Wing braces are the main structural member of a wing.

_____ 2. Torsion resists pulling forces.

_____ 3. Tensile strength is generally greater than or equal to shearing strength.

_____ 4. Longerons are the longitudinal members in a semimonocoque fuselage.

_____ 5. The benefit of a semimonocoque fuselage compared to a monocoque fuselage is that the semimonocoque fuselage does not require the skin to carry any load thereby reducing the stress on the skin.

_____ 6. Box beam wing constructions are used on transport category aircraft.

_____ 7. False ribs are those ribs which are used strictly for shaping the camber of the wing and do not provide any load support.

_____ 8. Cowlings are detachable panels which provide smooth airflow over the engine and protect it from damage.

_____ 9. Ribs can be lightened by stamping holes in the assembly.

_____ 10. High performance aircraft typically have fly-by-wire systems that utilize electrical power to move the elevators.

_____ 11. Fuel-carrying bladders located in a wing are known as wet wing designs.

_____ 12. Worm drives and flap tracks are used to move fowler flaps along their designed route of travel.

_____ 13. Leading edge flaps are independent of the trailing edge flaps.

_____ 14. Vortex generators are designed to reduce drag created by wingtip vortices.

_____ 15. Conventional gear and tricycle gear are interchangeable terms.

_____ 16. Aircraft equipped with pontoons or floats are sometimes known as amphibious aircraft

_____ 17. Water line measurements are perpendicular to the horizon.

_____ 18. Helicopters are moved horizontally by changing the angle of attack on the rotor blades.

_____ 19. Dissymmetry of lift causes blades to flutter.

_____ 20. Torque produced by the main rotors tries to spin the fuselage in the direction of blade rotation.

Chapter 1, Section A - Aircraft Structures

Name: _____ Date: _____

AIRCRAFT STRUCTURES

Section B
Knowledge Application Questions

1. Why are the rotors of a helicopter considered part of the airframe?

2. Define strain.

3. Describe stresses involved on a part being bent or subject to bending stress.

4. Cowlings and fairings do not require a high degree of strength but what characteristic is important for parts such as these?

5. What are the structural members that make up a truss-framed fuselage and what is it typically covered with?

6. What is the biggest problem associated with the monocoque type fuselage?

7. How is the monocoque type fuselage different than the semimonocoque type?

8. What causes metal fatigue in a pressurized aircraft fuselage structure?

9. When is the use of landing gear jury struts necessary and what purpose do they serve?

10. What is the function of the wing spar?

11. Where are false ribs located and what is their function?

AIRCRAFT STRUCTURES

12. Describe the characteristics of a nacelle and its components.

13. Directional control of a fixed-wing aircraft takes place around which axes? What are the respective control surfaces that move about these axes?

14. What affect does moving the aileron down have on the wing?

15. What are the functions of slots and where are they located?

16. How are balance tabs moved and what is their resulting effect?

17. What is the main benefit of conventional type landing gear?

18. Why are ground loops common on conventional landing gear?

19. Describe the cause(s) of dissymmetry of lift.

20. What is the NOTAR antitorque system and how does it work?

Chapter 1, Section B - Aircraft Structures

Name:_____   Date:_____

AIRCRAFT STRUCTURES

Section C
Final Chapter Exam

1. The material's internal resistance or counterforce that opposes deformation is called _____
   - ☐ A. rigidity.
   - ☐ B. strength.
   - ☐ C. stress.

2. What type of stress is a combination of compression and tension?
   - ☐ A. Torsion.
   - ☐ B. Shear.
   - ☐ C. Bending.

3. What type of construction method is used for most aluminum aircraft constructions?
   - ☐ A. Monocoque.
   - ☐ B. Semimonocoque.
   - ☐ C. Truss.

4. What is the angle called that is made between the fuselage and the horizontal plane of the wing?
   - ☐ A. Angle of attack.
   - ☐ B. Wing dihedral.
   - ☐ C. Angle of incidence.

5. How is the load transferred from the skin and the stringers to the spars?
   - ☐ A. Stiffeners.
   - ☐ B. Caps.
   - ☐ C. Ribs.

6. Where are wing butt ribs located?
   - ☐ A. Forward of the front spar.
   - ☐ B. In between the front and rear spar.
   - ☐ C. At the inboard edge of the wing.

7. What is the purpose of a fairing?
   - ☐ A. Allows for smooth airflow between the wing and fuselage.
   - ☐ B. Provide a strong and secure method for attaching the wing to the fuselage.
   - ☐ C. Receives compression loads that tend to force the wing spars together.

8. What are the names of the movable flight control surfaces on the empennage?
   - ☐ A. Horizontal Stabilizer and Elevator.
   - ☐ B. Vertical stabilizer and Rudder.
   - ☐ C. Elevator and Rudder.

9. What flight control surface movement causes the aircraft to roll?
   - ☐ A. Aileron.
   - ☐ B. Elevator.
   - ☐ C. Rudder.

10. What type of movement does the rudder control?
    - ☐ A. Roll.
    - ☐ B. Pitch.
    - ☐ C. Yaw.

11. What is a common design feature of ailerons to prevent flutter?
    - ☐ A. Hinge points aft of the leading edge.
    - ☐ B. Hinge points forward of the leading edge.
    - ☐ C. Hinge points at the leading edge.

AIRCRAFT STRUCTURES

12. As the aileron moves downward, what happens to the camber and lift respectively?
    - ☐ A. Camber increases, lift decreases.
    - ☐ B. Camber decreases, lift decreases.
    - ☐ C. Camber increases, lift increases.

13. How is the elevator controlled from the cockpit?
    - ☐ A. Side-to-side motion of the control yoke.
    - ☐ B. Push and pull motion of the control yoke.
    - ☐ C. Depressing of foot-operated pedals.

14. Which two types of control surfaces reduce the force needed to move a primary control surface?
    - ☐ A. Anti-balance and servo tabs.
    - ☐ B. Trim and balance tabs.
    - ☐ C. Slats and spoilers.

15. What type of secondary flight control decreases lift?
    - ☐ A. Slats.
    - ☐ B. Slots.
    - ☐ C. Spoilers.

16. Spoilers may be fully deployed on both wings at the same time for what purpose?
    - ☐ A. Augment aileron function.
    - ☐ B. Decrease lift inflight.
    - ☐ C. Speed brakes.

17. What flight control tabs move in the same direction as the control surface to which it is attached?
    - ☐ A. Trim.
    - ☐ B. Spring.
    - ☐ C. Anti-balance.

18. How are flight control surfaces moved on an aircraft that is equipped with a fly-by-wire system?
    - ☐ A. Electrical input only.
    - ☐ B. Hydraulic actuators and electrical input.
    - ☐ C. Control cables only.

19. What type of device is used as a barrier on the upper surface of the wing to reduce the tendency of the wing to stall at low flight speeds?
    - ☐ A. Stall Fence.
    - ☐ B. Vortex Generator.
    - ☐ C. Gap Seals.

20. Where is the center of gravity located on an aircraft with a tricycle landing gear?
    - ☐ A. Forward of the main wheels.
    - ☐ B. Aft of the main wheels.
    - ☐ C. Inline with the main wheels.

21. Fuselage stations are numbered in inches from _____
    - ☐ A. the buttock line.
    - ☐ B. the reference datum.
    - ☐ C. the water line.

22. _____ is a measurement forward or aft of the front spar and perpendicular to the water line.
    - ☐ A. Aileron station
    - ☐ B. Flap station
    - ☐ C. Nacelle station

AIRCRAFT STRUCTURES

23. How are main rotors of helicopters classified?
    - ☐ A. The transmission used to power the rotors.
    - ☐ B. Blade attachment and motion relative to the hub.
    - ☐ C. Swash plate and pitch change units attached to the blade.

24. How is the pitch of the rotor blades changed in a rigid rotor system?
    - ☐ A. Feathering Hinges.
    - ☐ B. Coning Hinges.
    - ☐ C. Teetering Hinges.

25. What is the windspeed and lift developed by the advancing blade in relation to the retreating blade?
    - ☐ A. Greater Windspeed, Less Lift.
    - ☐ B. Slower Windspeed, Less Lift.
    - ☐ C. Greater Windspeed, More Lift.

Chapter 1, Final Chapter Exam - Aircraft Structures

Name:_____   Date:_____

AIRCRAFT STRUCTURES

PAGE LEFT BLANK INTENTIONALLY

AERODYNAMICS, AIRCRAFT ASSEMBLY, AND RIGGING

CHAPTER 2

Section A
Study Aid Questions - Fill In The Blanks

1. The study of objects in motion through the air and the _____ governing that motion come from the Greek combination of "aero" and "_____".

2. Atmospheric pressure is measured inWW _____ with a _____.

3. As an aircraft descends atmospheric pressure _____, the amount of oxygen in the air _____, and temperature _____.

4. Density varies _____ with temperature and _____ with pressure.

5. A body at rest does not move unless a force is applied to it is Newton's _____ law and is known as the law of _____.

6. According to Bernoulli's principle, fluid flowing through a constriction experiences a(n) _____ in speed.

7. Velocity increases and pressure decreases on the _____ of the wing.

8. A pilot can increase the lift of an aircraft by increasing the _____.

9. The acute angle the wing chord makes with the _____ axis is called angle of incidence.

10. The boundary layer is the layer of _____ closest to the surface and its behavior is controlled in order to minimize _____ drag and skin friction drag.

11. Fluids always move from _____ to _____ pressure. This principle explains the spanwise movement of air flow from the bottom of the wing _____ and upward around the wing creating spillage over the wingtip called _____.

12. An object that tends to returns to equilibrium is said to have positive _____ stability.

13. _____ control the lateral movements of the aircraft, the _____ controls the longitudinal movements, and the _____ controls the directional movements.

14. An auto-gryo is an aircraft with a horizontal rotor that is _____ and turns due to the passage of air _____ through the rotor.

15. The blade with the decreased angle of attack tends to flap _____.

AERODYNAMICS, AIRCRAFT ASSEMBLY, AND RIGGING

16. The collective pitch control is operated with the _____ hand and is used to make pitch angle changes to _____ the main rotor blades.

17. There is a _____ of lift between the advancing and retreating blade.

18. Autorotation is possible through a freewheeling unit, a special _____ mechanism, which automatically disengages the engine in the event of its failure.

19. Helicopters with tandem rotors use the pedals to tilt the main rotors. When the _____ pedal is pushed forward the aft rotor moves to the _____.

20. Swaging tools generally have a _____ dimensions in an attempt to avoid defective or inferior swages.

21. Cables that travel completely through bulkheads require the use of a _____ and should not be deflected more than _____ from a straight line.

22. A groove or knurl around the end of the barrel of a _____ can be used to identify the _____ threads.

23. Structural alignment is the _____ the main structural component related to the longitudinal datum line parallel to the aircraft centerline and the lateral datum line parallel to the line joining the _____.

24. Hard landings and abnormal flight experiences prompt a check of the wing _____ and angle of _____.

25. The most common method of safety wiring is the _____ however; a _____ method can be used for smaller screws and tight spaces.

Section A
True of False

_____ 1. Air is considered a fluid.

_____ 2. Atmospheric pressure changes with altitude.

_____ 3. Aircraft can fly faster at lower altitudes because there is more pulling force from the engine cutting through the air.

_____ 4. Density varies directly with humidity.

_____ 5. Airflow over an airfoil can be explained using Bernoulli's principle and this pressure differential is called lift.

_____ 6. One wing can have numerous airfoil sections each with unique properties.

_____ 7. The efficiency of a wing is measured in terms of wing camber and AOA.

_____ 8. An aircraft has four forces acting upon it at all times: gravity, lift, thrust and weight.

AERODYNAMICS, AIRCRAFT ASSEMBLY, AND RIGGING

Section A
True of False

_____ 9. Induced drag increases as AOA increase.

_____ 10. Center of pressure has the greatest affect on the stability of an aircraft.

_____ 11. The vertical stabilizer is the primary surface that controls directional stability on the horizontal axis.

_____ 12. Trim tabs enable the pilot to correct any unbalanced condition that may exist during flight without touching the flight controls.

_____ 13. Canards are often used in swept wing aircraft to prevent spanwise air movements at high angles of attack.

_____ 14. Stick shakers were installed in hydromechanical flight control systems which provide an artificial stall warning.

_____ 15. At high forward speed a situation called retreating blade stall can occur because of the high AOA and slow relative wind speed.

_____ 16. Control surfaces must be rebalanced whenever there is weight added to a control surface.

_____ 17. The balance beam rebalancing method requires a specialized manufacturer made tool.

_____ 18. Lead and steel are the most common materials used to balance control surfaces.

_____ 19. The Type certification Data Sheet is issued by the manufacturer and includes information such as airspeed limitations, weight limits, and fuel type.

_____ 20. A 7×19 cable is very rigid and used for engine controls and trim tab controls.

_____ 21. Soldering cable ends is a common technique used to prevent fraying.

_____ 22. Cables are checked for corrosion by bending them.

_____ 23. A double-wrap safety wire method is preferred when securing a turnbuckle.

_____ 24. Rudder alignment is done by removing the controls surface from its hinges and passing a Plumb bob though the hinge attachment holes.

_____ 25. Cotter pins, unlike safety wire, can be reused.

Chapter 2, Section A - Aerodynamics, Aircraft Assembly, and Rigging

Name:_____   Date:_____

8083-31B-ATB Airframe Workbook

AERODYNAMICS, AIRCRAFT ASSEMBLY, AND RIGGING

PAGE LEFT BLANK INTENTIONALLY

AERODYNAMICS, AIRCRAFT ASSEMBLY, AND RIGGING

Section B
Knowledge Application Questions

1. Why is air considered a fluid?

2. What is atmospheric pressure and how is it measured?

3. What is the relationship between density, pressure, and temperature?

4. What is the difference between absolute humidity and relative humidity?

5. What is Newton's third law and what does it state?

6. Describe how Bernoulli's principle relates to a wing.

7. Describe what happens to the resultant force as the AOA increases.

8. Describe the other force produced besides lift as the relative motion of the air moves over the wing.

9. What does control and controllability mean for a pilot and the aircraft?

10. Explain the aerodynamic effect that occurs at and above the speed of sound.

11. Explain what fully articulated means in relation to a helicopter rotor system.

AERODYNAMICS, AIRCRAFT ASSEMBLY, AND RIGGING

12. How does Newton's third law relate to helicopters?

13. Explain what a correlator is and what it does.

14. What are the most common causes of high frequency vibrations?

15. Why is no clutch necessary on a helicopter engine with a free turbine?

16. Describe the use of pulleys and pulley guards.

17. Control cable rigging generally consists of what three steps?

18. What is the purpose of a turnbuckle?

19. Where are cable drums typically found and what do they do?

20. What are the types of inspection programs helicopter operates use in accordance with 14 CFR part 91?

Chapter 2, Section B - Aerodynamics, Aircraft Assembly, and Rigging

Name:_____   Date:_____

AERODYNAMICS, AIRCRAFT ASSEMBLY, AND RIGGING

Section C
Final Chapter Exam

1. What happens to the pressure of a fluid in a container when it is heated?
   - ☐ A. Pressure increases.
   - ☐ B. Pressure decreases.
   - ☐ C. Pressure remains the same.

2. A wing with a high fineness ratio has which of the following characteristics?
   - ☐ A. Thin wing, small amount of skin friction.
   - ☐ B. Thick wing, small amount of skin friction.
   - ☐ C. Thin wing, large amount of skin friction.

3. Exposed aircraft components create resistance known as _____
   - ☐ A. parasite drag.
   - ☐ B. skin friction drag.
   - ☐ C. induced drag.

4. _____ is the quality of the response of an aircraft to the pilot's commands during maneuvers.
   - ☐ A. Stability.
   - ☐ B. Controllability.
   - ☐ C. Maneuverability.

5. Which axis extends from nose to tail?
   - ☐ A. Vertical axis.
   - ☐ B. Lateral axis.
   - ☐ C. Longitudinal axis.

6. What type of stability can be artificially increased with a yaw dampener?
   - ☐ A. Directional.
   - ☐ B. Dynamic.
   - ☐ C. Dutch roll.

7. Which of the following type of aircraft structures reduce fuel consumption and increases range?
   - ☐ A. Wing fences.
   - ☐ B. Winglets.
   - ☐ C. Both A & B.

8. Compressible aerodynamics deals with speeds at _____
   - ☐ A. Wing fences.
   - ☐ B. Winglets.
   - ☐ C. Vortex generators.

9. What type of rotor is found on aircraft with dual rotor blades?
   - ☐ A. Fully articulated.
   - ☐ B. Semi rigid.
   - ☐ C. Rigid.

10. Drift in the direction of the tail rotor during hover is called _____
    - ☐ A. ground effect.
    - ☐ B. translational tendency.
    - ☐ C. translational lift.

11. Effective translational lift is experienced at what airspeed?
    - ☐ A. Between hover and 16 knots.
    - ☐ B. Between 16-24 knots.
    - ☐ C. 24 knots and above.

AERODYNAMICS, AIRCRAFT ASSEMBLY, AND RIGGING

12. A helicopter with counterclockwise rotating main rotor would experience which of the following conditions if dissymmetry of lift were allowed to exist with no corrective action?
    - ☐ A. Roll to the left.
    - ☐ B. Roll to the right.
    - ☐ C. Drift to the left.

13. How does a pilot compensate for blowback?
    - ☐ A. Move the cyclic forward.
    - ☐ B. Move the cyclic aft.
    - ☐ C. Pull up on the collective.

14. What component transmits the control inputs from the collective and cyclic to the main rotor blades?
    - ☐ A. Transmission.
    - ☐ B. Control rod.
    - ☐ C. Swash plate.

15. Where is the throttle control located in a helicopter?
    - ☐ A. On the collective.
    - ☐ B. On the cyclic.
    - ☐ C. On a lever next to the collective.

16. What is the primary purpose of the helicopter main rotor transmission?
    - ☐ A. Increase engine output RPM to optimum rotor RPM.
    - ☐ B. Decrease engine output RPM to optimum rotor RPM.
    - ☐ C. Synchronize the rotation of the engine with the rotor.

17. During static balancing, an upward movement of the trailing edge of a control surface on a balance stand indicates _____
    - ☐ A. an overbalance designated with a (+) sign.
    - ☐ B. an underbalance designated with a (-) sign.
    - ☐ C. an overbalance designated with a (-) sign.

18. Which rebalancing method can be performed without removing the control surface from the aircraft?
    - ☐ A. Calculation method.
    - ☐ B. Scale method.
    - ☐ C. Balance beam method.

19. _____ may be used to force the primary nut thread against the bolt or screw thread.
    - ☐ A. A lock nut
    - ☐ B. A lock washer
    - ☐ C. A pal nut

20. ELT tests should be conducted _____
    - ☐ A. during the last 5 minutes of any hour.
    - ☐ B. during the first 5 minutes of any hour.
    - ☐ C. during the first 15 minutes of any hour.

21. The control surface used to increase or decrease an aircraft's angle of attack is _____
    - ☐ A. an aileron.
    - ☐ B. an elevator.
    - ☐ C. a flap.

22. What are the primary flight controls?
    - ☐ A. Ailerons, elevators, and rudder.
    - ☐ B. Ailerons, elevators, and flaps.
    - ☐ C. Ailerons, rudder, and spoilers.

AERODYNAMICS, AIRCRAFT ASSEMBLY, AND RIGGING

23. What are Balance tabs?
    - ☐ A. Aid in moving the main control surface.
    - ☐ B. Are designed to move in the opposite direction of the primary flight control.
    - ☐ C. Are used for the same purpose as hydraulic actuators.

24. What is included in the Auxiliary lift group?
    - ☐ A. Flaps, slats, and slots.
    - ☐ B. Flaps, aileron trim, and speed brakes.
    - ☐ C. Slats, slots, and elevator spring tabs.

25. What kind of devices decrease lift?
    - ☐ A. Flaps, ailerons, speed brakes.
    - ☐ B. Speed brakes and spoilers.
    - ☐ C. Speed brakes, slots, slats.

Chapter 2, Final Chapter Exam - Aerodynamics, Aircraft Assembly, and Rigging

Name:_____   Date:_____

AERODYNAMICS, AIRCRAFT ASSEMBLY, AND RIGGING

PAGE LEFT BLANK INTENTIONALLY

AIRCRAFT FABRIC COVERING

CHAPTER 3

Section A
Study Aid Questions - Fill In The Blanks

1. Organic fabrics, like linen and _____, were the original fabrics used for covering airframes but their tendency to _____ gave way to a process known as _____.

2. Organic fabrics generally only last _____ years.

3. _____ fabric is the standard covering currently being used in the United States.

4. Pinked edges have been cut into a continuous series of V's by machine or special _____ to prevent _____.

5. Deviations from the supplemental type certificate in any way renders the aircraft _____.

6. A _____ field approval may be acquired to deviate from the original covering process or material.

7. _____ is the single most destructive element that causes polyester fabric to deteriorate.

8. To achieve a level and deep glossy finish, _____ is added to slow dry time.

9. Finishing tape is used to cover all _____ and rib lacing to provide a smooth finish and _____.

10. Fungicide and mildewicide are only required for _____ fabric.

11. Loose fabric affects the _____ distribution and _____ the airframe.

12. A _____ may be used per the manufacturer's instruction if the dope coating is found to have cracks but the fabric itself is still _____.

13. Breaking strength is determined by cutting a test strip, taken from an area that is _____ to the elements, which is _____ by 4-6 inches.

14. The _____ method of re-covering uses multiple flat sections of fabric attached to the frame whereas the envelope method uses _____ envelopes to cover the aircraft.

15. It's important in the re-covering process that the _____, _____, and ventilation be controlled.

16. Fabric coatings should be applied with a high-_____, low-_____ sprayer.

17. Some of the primary concerns of fabric seams are strength, elasticity, _____ and good _____.

AIRCRAFT FABRIC COVERING

18. Closer spacing of rib lacing should be done in the area that experiences _____, about one propeller width plus _____.

19. Inspection rings are left intact and only removed when _____ is required. It is then closed using preformed _____ panels.

20. Fabric gussets, installed as _____, reinforce cable guide openings and _____-attached fitting areas.

Section A
True of False

_____ 1. Warp describes the direction across the width of the fabric.

_____ 2. The same materials and techniques must be used when replacing aircraft fabric.

_____ 3. A TSO is a technical standard order issued by the manufacturer for specific parts, materials, processes, and appliances use on civil aircraft.

_____ 4. Only companies with a PMA may manufacture and sell aviation fabric.

_____ 5. The same thread may be used to hand sew and machine sew aviation fabric.

_____ 6. Prior to airframe covering, the structure must be primed.

_____ 7. Fabric cement is used to attach the fabric to the airframe.

_____ 8. Fabric is still airworthy down to 70% of the breaking strength of new fabric.

_____ 9. Fabric test strips should have all the coatings left on to get an accurate measurement of the fabric's breaking strength.

_____ 10. Punch testers like Seyboth and Maule give an accurate representation of the fabric breaking strength.

_____ 11. The Maule punch tester does not puncture airworthy fabric during testing.

_____ 12. Fuselage and wings can be covered with one large envelope.

_____ 13. Many of the substances used to re-cover an aircraft are highly toxic.

_____ 14. Old adhesive stuck to the airframe can be removed with MEK.

_____ 15. Polyester fabric generally incorporates sewn seams.

_____ 16. An ordinary household iron may be used to heat shrink fabric.

_____ 17. Heat shrinking should be done evenly by starting from one end and progressing to the other end.

_____ 18. Finishing tape is applied to all seams, edges, and ribs.

_____ 19. Wing leading edges usually receive the narrowest amount of finishing tape to reduce irregularities during the covering process.

_____ 20. There is no compromise in strength between cemented repairs and sewn repairs.

Chapter 3, Section A - Aircraft Fabric Covering

Name:_____   Date:_____

AIRCRAFT FABRIC COVERING

Section B
Knowledge Application Questions

1. How do aircraft designers address the flammability of nitrate doping and the process they use for its application?

2. Explain why replacing cotton fabric with polyester fabric on an aircraft is considered a major alteration.

3. Describe what anti-chafe tape is and when it is used.

4. Explain the process of re-covering an aircraft using the blanket method.

5. What are some of the necessary personal protection equipment needed when re-covering an aircraft?

6. What is used to produce a smooth finish on leading edges of aluminum wings? What is essential when considering this process?

7. Describe the process of heat shrinking fabric.

8. What is the purpose of a drain grommet and where are they located?

9. How are finishing tapes applied at the leading and trailing edges?

AIRCRAFT FABRIC COVERING

10. What is fabric primer and what does it do?

11. What two types of fabric are used for covering aircraft?

12. What are the organic fibers used for covering aircraft?

13. What are the synthetic fibers used for covering aircraft?

14. What determines the quality and strength requirements for a fabric-covered aircraft?

15. What strength of fabric should be used for re-covering an aircraft?

16. What is a fabric selvage edge?

17. What is the purpose of reinforcing tape?

18. How are ventilation and drainage hole edges reinforced?

19. What is one advantage of the envelope method of covering wings?

AIRCRAFT FABRIC COVERING

20. What rib lace spacing is used when the original spacing is unknown?

21. What is a tie-off knot?

22. What is the purpose of a fabric rejuvenator?

23. What methods are used to check the condition of doped fabric?

24. What is the maximum permissible deterioration for used aircraft fabric?

25. What type of fabric is not affected by moisture and mildew?

Chapter 3, Section B - Aircraft Fabric Covering

Name:_____   Date:_____

AIRCRAFT FABRIC COVERING

PAGE LEFT BLANK INTENTIONALLY

AIRCRAFT FABRIC COVERING

Section C
Final Chapter Exam

1. What does the term bias mean in relation to fabric coverings?
   - ☐ A. The weave across the width of the fabric.
   - ☐ B. The warp along the direction of the fabric.
   - ☐ C. A cut or fold made at a diagonal to the warp.

2. Which 14 CFR part 43 Appendix states what maintenance actions are considered minor and major repairs?
   - ☐ A. A
   - ☐ B. B
   - ☐ C. C

3. Major fabric repairs need to be inspected by _____
   - ☐ A. airframe mechanic.
   - ☐ B. airframe and powerplant mechanic.
   - ☐ C. airframe and powerplant mechanic with an inspection authorization.

4. Where is reinforcing tape most commonly used?
   - ☐ A. Seams.
   - ☐ B. Rib caps.
   - ☐ C. Around inspection rings.

5. Which of the following is used to create reinforced drain holes in aircraft fabric?
   - ☐ A. Inspection rings.
   - ☐ B. Spring clips.
   - ☐ C. Grommets.

6. What type of coating is applied to protect the fabric from UV light?
   - ☐ A. Primer.
   - ☐ B. Sealer.
   - ☐ C. Filler.

7. When is accelerator used when applying fabric topcoats?
   - ☐ A. Temperatures below ideal working temperatures.
   - ☐ B. Temperatures above ideal working temperatures.
   - ☐ C. Humidity above ideal working conditions.

8. What is the key ingredient in the Poly-Fiber covering system?
   - ☐ A. Polyurethane.
   - ☐ B. Vinyl.
   - ☐ C. Water-based glue.

9. Aircraft with wing loading of 9 lb/ft² and over should have fabric strength at or above _____
   - ☐ A. Grade A.
   - ☐ B. intermediate grade.
   - ☐ C. lightweight.

10. Aircraft with a VNE of 135 mph or less are considered to be unairworthy when the fabric breaking strength has deteriorated to below _____
    - ☐ A. 56.
    - ☐ B. 46.
    - ☐ C. 35.

11. Re-covering a fabric aircraft is considered _____
    - ☐ A. A minor repair or alteration.
    - ☐ B. A major repair or alteration.
    - ☐ C. General maintenance.

AIRCRAFT FABRIC COVERING

12. Which fabric covering system is nonhazardous?
    - ☐ A. Superflite.
    - ☐ B. Air-Tech.
    - ☐ C. Stewart.

13. Critical airflow areas such as the leading edge require how many inches of overlap at the seam?
    - ☐ A. 1-2
    - ☐ B. 2-4
    - ☐ C. 4-6

14. How much does polyester fabric shrink at 350°F?
    - ☐ A. 5%
    - ☐ B. 8%
    - ☐ C. 10%

15. Which of the following repairs require sewing?
    - ☐ A. Cotton Fabric repairs.
    - ☐ B. Polyester fabric repairs.
    - ☐ C. Fiberglass fabric repairs.

16. Where can technicians find instructions about tying the correct knots during the rib lacing process?
    - ☐ A. STC and maintenance manuals.
    - ☐ B. AC43-7B.
    - ☐ C. Type Certificate Data Sheet.

17. What should be applied to rib caps that are not rounded over?
    - ☐ A. Anti-chafe tape.
    - ☐ B. Reinforcing tape.
    - ☐ C. Surface tape.

18. How many blankets does it usually take to cover a wing?
    - ☐ A. 1
    - ☐ B. 2
    - ☐ C. At least 4.

19. Which of the following is a FAA approved method of testing fabric?
    - ☐ A. Mechanical fabric strength testers.
    - ☐ B. Visual inspection.
    - ☐ C. NDT inspection.

20. Which of the following fabrics is no longer available?
    - ☐ A. Grade A cotton.
    - ☐ B. Lightweight polyester.
    - ☐ C. Ceconite 101.

21. Which tape is already preshrunk?
    - ☐ A. Anti-chafe tape.
    - ☐ B. Rib bracing tape.
    - ☐ C. Surface tape.

22. What additive increases the overall flexibility and life of a coating?
    - ☐ A. Thinner.
    - ☐ B. Retarder.
    - ☐ C. Rejuvenator.

23. Finishing tape (surface tape) is used for what purpose?
    - ☐ A. To help prevent 'ripple formation' in covering fabric.
    - ☐ B. To provide additional anti-tear resistance under reinforcement tape.
    - ☐ C. To provide additional wear resistance over the edges of fabric forming structures.

24. The determining factor(s) for the selection of the correct weight of textile fabric to be used in covering any type of aircraft is the Re-covering
   ☐ A. maximum wing loading.
   ☐ B. speed of the aircraft.
   ☐ C. speed of the aircraft and the maximum wing loading.

25. Any protrusions in the fabric covering are reinforced with _____
   ☐ A. rings.
   ☐ B. grommets.
   ☐ C. gussets.

AIRCRAFT FABRIC COVERING

PAGE LEFT BLANK INTENTIONALLY

AIRCRAFT METAL STRUCTURAL REPAIR

CHAPTER 4

Section A
Study Aid Questions - Fill In The Blanks

1. A joint that is too weak cannot be tolerated, but neither can one that is too _____ because it can create stress risers that may cause _____ in other locations.

2. There are six types of stresses: tension, compression, _____ , and bearing are known as basic stresses; while bending and _____ (or twisting) are considered combination stresses.

3. There are two ways to determine rivet size: (1) the size of rivets in the next _____ rivet row inboard on the wing and (2) multiple the thickness of the thickest sheet by _____ and use the next larger size.

4. Aircraft structural joint design involves an attempt to find the optimum strength relationship between being critical in _____ and critical in _____ .

5. A file with a single row of _____ teeth is called a single-cut file; whereas files with one row of teeth crossing under another row are called _____ files.

6. Files are classified according to their _____ . The most common files include: flat, triangle, square, _____ , and round.

7. _____ drill motors are recommended for use on projects around flammable materials where potentials spark from a(n) _____ drill motor might become a fire hazard.

8. Properly adjusted drill _____ can prevent excessive drill penetration that might damage the _____ structure or injure personnel.

9. A bar folder is designed for use in making _____ or folds along edges of sheet metal.

10. _____ breaks are used to form thicker more _____ parts.

11. On the slip roll, the front rollers _____ or grip the metal sheet while the rear roll provides the proper _____ to the work.

12. It is advantageous to _____ or even polish the edges of a flange that must undergo even moderate _____ to avoid crack formation.

13. _____ made of hardwood are widely used in airframe metalwork for shrinking and stretching metal, particularly angles and _____ .

14. The minimum bend radius is affected by; the kind of material, _____ of the material, and _____ condition of the material.

15. The _____ must be used for all bend that are smaller or larger than _____ .

AIRCRAFT METAL STRUCTURAL REPAIR

16. In order to form a box, it is necessary to drill _____ at the intersection of the inside bend _____ lines.

17. Machining characteristics of magnesium are _____, making possible the use of maximum speeds of the machine tools with heavy cuts and high _____ rates.

18. Rivets fill the hole during the installation process which provides a good _____ transfer.

19. Blind rivets are installed during _____ where access is not available to form the driven head of _____ rivets.

20. The Cherry-MAX® rivet consists of five parts; _____ blind header, hollow rivet shell, _____ collar, driving anvil, and the pulling stem.

21. Collars used with Hi-Lok fasteners have a _____ break-off groove which shears off at a predetermined _____, leaving the lower portion of the collar seated with the proper torque.

22. An interference fit is typically used for _____ and _____ fit is used for steel, titanium, and composites.

23. Rivnuts are internally threaded _____ that have a flush or shallow _____ heads.

24. Rivet diameter should not be _____ than 3 times the thickness of the _____.

25. Rivet _____ is the distance between the centers of _____ rivets in the same row.

26. If countersinking is done on metal below a certain thickness a _____ with less than minimum bearing surface or _____ of the hole may occur.

27. A rivet gun with the correct header must be held snugly against the head and _____ to the surface while the bucking bar of the proper _____ is held against the opposite end.

28. _____ repair is very important because of the load it carries and particular care should be taken to ensure the original _____ of the structure is not impaired.

29. A scale or _____ can be used to check the condition of the upset rivet head to see that it conforms to the proper requirements.

30. _____ dimpling is the process that uses heated dimpling dies so that the material will _____ better during the dimpling process.

Chapter 4, Section A - Aircraft Metal Structural Repair

Name: _____ Date: _____

AIRCRAFT METAL STRUCTURAL REPAIR

Section B
Knowledge Application

1. Identify each of the statements and figures below: (answers may be used more than once)

   A. Tension
   B. Compression
   C. Shear
   D. Bearing
   E. Torsion
   F. Bending

   _____ 1. The force that resists the force that rivets or bolts place on a hole.

   _____ 2. The force per unit area which causes adjacent particles of material to slide past each other.

   _____ 3. A combination of two forces acting upon a structural member at one or more points.

   _____ 4. The force which tends to twist a structural member.

   _____ 5. The force per unit area which tends to stretch a structural member.

   _____ 6. The force per unit area which tends to shorten a structural member at any cross section.

   _____ 7.

   _____ 10.

   _____ 8.

   _____ 11.

   _____ 9.

8083-31B-ATB Airframe Workbook

AIRCRAFT METAL STRUCTURAL REPAIR

Matching

2. Match to each of the statements below:

   A. Brinelling   E. Crack   I. Chattering   M. Nick   Q. Stain
   B. Burnishing   F. Cut   J. Galling   N. Pitting R. Upsetting
   C. Burr   G. Dent   K. Gouge   O. Scratch
   D. Corrosion   H. Erosion   L. Inclusion   P. Score

   _____ 1. Presence of foreign or extraneous material wholly within a portion of metal.

   _____ 2. A small, thin section of metal extending beyond a regular surface.

   _____ 3. Breakdown or deterioration of metal surface by vibratory action.

   _____ 4. A change in color, locally causing a noticeably different appearance.

   _____ 5. Loss of metal, usually to an appreciable depth over a relatively long, narrow area.

   _____ 6. Occurrence of shallow, spherical depressions in a surface.

   _____ 7. A physical separation of two adjacent portions of metal.

   _____ 8. Slight tear or break in metal surface from light contact by a foreign object.

   _____ 9. Indentation in a metal surface produced by an object striking with force.

   _____ 10. Loss of metal from the surface by chemical or electrochemical action.

   _____ 11. Deep tear or break in metal surface from contact under pressure.

   _____ 12. Breakdown of metal surfaces due to excessive friction between two part.

   _____ 13. Local break or notch on edge.

   _____ 14. A displacement of material beyond the normal contour or surface.

   _____ 15. Polishing of one surface by sliding contact with a smooth, hard surface.

   _____ 16. Loss of metal from the surface by mechanical action of foreign object.

   _____ 17. Sharp, localized breakdown of metal surface with defined edges.

   _____ 18. Grooves in a metal surface from contact with foreign material under heavy pressure.

3. Match to each of the statements below:

   A. Scales   D. Rivet Spacer   G. Punches
   B. Combination Square E. Marking Tool   H. Awls
   C. Dividers   F. Scribes   I. Hole Duplicator

   _____ 1. Makes quick and accurate rivet pattern layouts on a sheet.

   _____ 2. Only used when marks will be removed by drilling or cutting.

   _____ 3. A scale with three heads that can be moved to any position on the scale.

   _____ 4. A carbon steel tempered marking tool.

   _____ 5. Comes in lengths most commonly 6" and 12".

   _____ 6. Used to locate and match existing holes in structures.

   _____ 7. Fiber tipped pen.

   _____ 8. Used in aircraft maintenance to align holes.

   _____ 9. Transfer measurement from a device to a scale to determine its value.

AIRCRAFT METAL STRUCTURAL REPAIR

Matching

4. Match to each of the statements below:

   A. Prick Punch C. Automatic Center Punch E. Pin Punch G. Chassis Punch
   B. Center Punch D. Transfer Punch F. Drive Punch

   _____ 1. Has an adjustable cap for regulating the stroke.

   _____ 2. Used to transfer dimensions from a paper pattern directly onto metal.

   _____ 3. Also known as a drift punch.

   _____ 4. Used to mark the locations of new holes using a template or existing holes.

   _____ 5. Used to make holes in sheet metal.

   _____ 6. Used to make large indentations in metal for a twist drill.

   _____ 7. Used to drive out damaged rivets, pins and bolts.

5. Match the names to the figure below:

   _____ 1. Body

   _____ 2. Land

   _____ 3. Cutting Lips

   _____ 4. Notched Point Chisel Edges

   _____ 5. Flute

   _____ 6. Shank

6. Match to each of the statements below:

   A. Leg   E. Neutral Axis   I. Setback   M. Closed Angle
   B. Flange   F. Mold Line   J. Flat   N. Open Angle
   C. Grain Of Metal G. Mold Point   K. Bend Allowance   O. K-Factor
   D. Bend Radius   H. Bend Tangent Line   L. Bend Line   P. Total Developed

   _____ 1. Located where the metal starts to bend and the metal stops curving.

   _____ 2. Set even with the nose of the brake and acts as a guide for bending.

   _____ 3. Measured from a radius center to the inside surface of the metal.

   _____ 4. Width of material, measured around the bends from edge to edge.

   _____ 5. The distance from the mold point to the bend tangent line.

   _____ 6. Angle that is more than 90° when measured between legs.

   _____ 7. Line formed by extending the outside surface of the leg and flange to a point in space.

   _____ 8. The longer part of a formed angle.

   _____ 9. Curved section of metal within the bend.

   _____ 10. The shorter part of a formed angle.

   _____ 11. Corresponds to one of the angles to which metal can be bent.

   _____ 12. An imaginary line that has the same length after bending as it had before.

   _____ 13. The base measurement minus setback (=MLD-SB).

   _____ 14. The point of intersection of the mold lines.

   _____ 15. Angle that is more than 90° when the amount of bend is measured.

   _____ 16. Bend should preferably be made to lie at an angle to this width.

AIRCRAFT METAL STRUCTURAL REPAIR

7. Match to each of the statements and figures below:

    A. Universal Head

    B. Modified Universal Head

    C. Standard 100° Flush Head

    D. Reduced Flush Head

    E. Modified 120° Countersink

    F. Cherry Hollow End E-Z Buck

    _____ 1. Designed specifically for double-flush applications.

    _____ 2. Are not to be used where aerodynamics is a factor.

    _____ 3. Designed to limit rivet tipping.

    _____ 4. Replacement for both round and brazier head rivets.

    _____ 5. Sacrifice clamp-up strength for increased shear strength.

    _____ 6. Ideal for dimpling.

8. Match the names to the figure below:

    A. 1100 Aluminum
    B. 5056 Aluminum
    C. 2117 Aluminum
    D. 2017 Aluminum
    E. 2024 Aluminum
    F. 7050 Aluminum
    G. Monel

    _____ 1.   _____ 3.   _____ 5.   _____ 7.

    _____ 2.   _____ 4.   _____ 6.

    _____ 8. Alloy Code-E

    _____ 9. Alloy Code-AD

    _____ 10. Alloy Code-M

    _____ 11. Alloy Code-DD

    _____ 12. Alloy Code-B

    _____ 13. Alloy Code-A

9. Fill in the boxes:

Minimum Edge Distance

Edge Distance/Edge Margin	Minimum Edge Distance	Preferred Edge Distance
Protruding Head Rivets	1.	2.
Countersunk Rivets	3.	4.

AIRCRAFT METAL STRUCTURAL REPAIR

10. Fill in the boxes:

Rivet Pitch/Spacing

Rivet Spacing	Minimum Edge Distance	Preferred Edge Distance
1 and 3 Row Protruding Head Rivet Layout	1.	2.
2 Row Protruding Head Rivet Layout	3.	4.
1 and 3 Rows Countersunk Head Rivet Layout	5.	6.
2 Row Countersunk Head Rivet Layout	7.	8.

11. What is done with the rivet head stem when a self plugging (friction lock) rivet is installed?

12. When do you need to use the K factor?

13. What calculation must be made when bending sheet metal?

14. What methods are used in forming sheet metal?

15. What is a tolerance?

16. Whenever possible the technician should use what types of materials for aircraft repairs?

AIRCRAFT METAL STRUCTURAL REPAIR

17. What is edge distance?

18. Why is a crack stop drilled before a repair is made?

19. How do you calculate the correct length of a rivet?

20. Describe rivet head markings for A, B, D, AD, and DD rivets.

Chapter 4, Section B - Aircraft Metal Structural Repair

Name:_____ Date:_____

Section C
Final Chapter Exam

1. Repairs must accomplish which of the following _____
   - ☐ A. accept stresses, carry them across the repair, and dissipate them in the appropriate area.
   - ☐ B. accept stresses, carry them across the repair, and transfer them back to the original structure.
   - ☐ C. accept stresses and disperse them throughout the repair.

2. What is needed when control surface repairs alter the weight distribution?
   - ☐ A. Counter-balance weight is added.
   - ☐ B. Balance weights are removed or added.
   - ☐ C. Balancing patches are used.

3. What must be done after holes are drilled in aluminum sheet metal?
   - ☐ A. Reamed.
   - ☐ B. Deburred.
   - ☐ C. Sanded.

4. What is the function of lubricants when drilling?
   - ☐ A. Assist in chip removal.
   - ☐ B. Deburr the holes.
   - ☐ C. Countersink the holes.

5. Straight line forming machines include all of the following except _____
   - ☐ A. bar folder.
   - ☐ B. combination break.
   - ☐ C. box and pan break.

6. What is needed for the press break to bend narrow U-channels?
   - ☐ A. Gooseneck dies.
   - ☐ B. Offset dies.
   - ☐ C. The press break cannot bend narrow U-channels.

7. What objects can a box and pan break form that a cornice break cannot?
   - ☐ A. Box.
   - ☐ B. Narrow U-channel.
   - ☐ C. Hat channel stringers.

8. What is an excellent technique for avoiding stresses at the edge of a part?
   - ☐ A. Use shims to avoid direct clamping on the part.
   - ☐ B. Deburring the edges of the part before bending.
   - ☐ C. Use mild steel instead of annealed aluminum.

9. What is used to support the bumping process?
   - ☐ A. Anvil.
   - ☐ B. Sandbag.
   - ☐ C. Dies.

10. What is the function of lubricants when drilling?
    - ☐ A. Assist in chip removal.
    - ☐ B. Deburr the holes.
    - ☐ C. Countersink the holes.

11. For calculation purposes, where is the neutral axis located in terms of thickness?
    - ☐ A. .5T
    - ☐ B. .445T
    - ☐ C. .545T

AIRCRAFT METAL STRUCTURAL REPAIR

12. What is the minimum bend radius of a .063" thick piece of 6061-T6 aluminum alloy? (*Refer to table below.*)
    - ☐ A. .16
    - ☐ B. .12
    - ☐ C. .44

Minimum Bend Radius for Aluminum Alloys						
THICKNESS	5052-0 6061-0 5052-H32	7178-0 2024-0 5052-H34 6061-T4 7075-0	6061-T6	7075-T6	2024-T3 2024-T4	2024-T6
.012	.03	.03	.03	.03	.06	.06
.016	.03	.03	.03	.03	.09	.09
.020	.03	.03	.03	.12	.09	.09
.025	.03	.03	.06	.16	.12	.09
.032	.03	.03	.06	.19	.12	.12
.040	.06	.06	.09	.22	.16	.16
.050	.06	.06	.12	.25	.19	.19
.063	.06	.09	.16	.31	.22	.25
.071	.09	.12	.16	.38	.25	.31
.080	.09	.16	.19	.44	.31	.38
.090	.09	.19	.22	.50	.38	.44
.100	.12	.22	.25	.62	.44	.50
.125	.12	.25	.31	.88	.50	.62
.160	.16	.31	.44	1.25	.75	.75
.190	.19	.38	.56	1.38	1.00	1.00
.250	.31	.62	.75	2.00	1.25	1.25
.312	.44	1.25	1.38	2.50	1.50	1.50
.375	.44	1.38	1.50	2.50	1.88	1.88

BEND RADIUS IS DESIGNATED TO THE INSIDE OF THE BEND. ALL DIMENSIONS ARE IN INCHES.

13. The distance between the two bends of a joggle is called the _____
    - ☐ A. neutral axis.
    - ☐ B. allowance.
    - ☐ C. J-intersection.

14. What can be done to prevent cracking in the bend area when bending CRES?
    - ☐ A. Use a bend radius smaller than recommended in the minimum bend radius table.
    - ☐ B. Use a bend radius larger than recommended in the minimum bend radius table.
    - ☐ C. Heat the CRES before bending.

15. What rivets are used for joining corrosion resistant steel and titanium parts together?
    - ☐ A. 7050 Aluminum.
    - ☐ B. 5056 Aluminum.
    - ☐ C. Monel.

16. Cherry-MAX® rivets are manufactured with which of the following head styles?
    - ☐ A. Universal, NAS 1097, 120° flush head.
    - ☐ B. Universal, NAS 1097, 130° flush head.
    - ☐ C. Universal, 100° flush head, 130° flush head.

17. What is an advantage of a Hi-lok fastener?
    - ☐ A. Inability to be overtorqued, light weight, high strength.
    - ☐ B. High strength, high fatigue resistance, low strength.
    - ☐ C. Light weight, high strength, low fatigue resistance.

AIRCRAFT METAL STRUCTURAL REPAIR

18. Which of the following is a permanent type fastener assembly that consists of a pin and collar?
    - ☐ A. Cherry-Buck®
    - ☐ B. Taper-Lok®
    - ☐ C. Eddie-Bolt®

19. What does a correct rivet installation require?
    - ☐ A. Dimpling of the skin, good hole preparations, removal of burrs.
    - ☐ B. Good hole preparations, removal of burrs, clamping the sheets together.
    - ☐ C. Countersinking holes, removal of burrs, dimpling of the skin.

20. Transverse pitch is the perpendicular distance between rivet rows and is usually equal to _____
    - ☐ A. 50% of the rivet pitch.
    - ☐ B. 75% of the rivet pitch.
    - ☐ C. 90% of the rivet pitch.

21. When using a rivet size of 1/8", what drill size should be used?
    - ☐ A. #40
    - ☐ B. #30
    - ☐ C. #21

22. Which of the following is not a common type of countersunk well?
    - ☐ A. 82°
    - ☐ B. 120°
    - ☐ C. 110°

23. The NACA riveting method has primary applications in _____
    - ☐ A. leading edge areas.
    - ☐ B. trailing edge areas.
    - ☐ C. fuel tank areas.

24. What is the purpose of refrigerating 2017 and 2024 aluminum alloy rivets after heat treatment?
    - ☐ A. To accelerate age hardening.
    - ☐ B. To relieve internal stresses.
    - ☐ C. To retard age hardening.

25. The dimensions of an MS20470AD-4-8 rivet are _____
    - ☐ A. 1/8 inch in diameter and 1/4 inch long.
    - ☐ B. 1/8 inch in diameter and 1/2 inch long.
    - ☐ C. 4/16 inch in diameter and 8/32 inch long.

Chapter 4, Final Chapter Exam - Aircraft Metal Structural Repair

Name:_____ Date:_____

AIRCRAFT METAL STRUCTURAL REPAIR

PAGE LEFT BLANK INTENTIONALLY

AIRCRAFT WELDING

CHAPTER 5

Section A
Study Aid Questions - Fill In The Blanks

1. There are 3 types of welding: _____, _____ and, _____ welding.

2. The oxy-acetylene flame, with a temperature of _____ Fahrenheit is produced with a torch burning _____ and mixing it with _____.

3. Shielded metal arc welding is the most common type and often referred to as _____ welding.

4. Gas Metal Arc Welding (GMAW) was formerly called _____.

5. When welding mild steel, stainless steel, or titanium the welder setting needs to be set to _____. When welding aluminum and magnesium _____ must be selected.

6. Electric resistance welding, either _____ or _____ welding is typically used to join thin sheet metal components.

7. The gas used with Plasma Arc Welding is _____. The torch also uses secondary gas such as _____ or _____ that assists in shielding the puddle.

8. Argon is _____, _____, _____ and non-toxic.

9. The oxygen hose is _____ and has _____ threads indicated by the absence of a groove.

10. The size of the tip opening not _____ determines how much heat is applied to the work.

11. All cylinders should be stored and transported in the _____ position, especially acetylene because they contain an absorbent material saturated with _____.

12. The higher the welding tip number the _____ the hole in the tip.

13. Three flame types flame commonly used for welding are _____, _____, and _____.

14. The oxidizing flame burns at approximately _____ °F and is produced by burning an excess of _____.

15. A _____ may be caused by touching the tip to the work, _____ the tip, by a _____ tip, or by dirt or slag in the end of the tip.

16. Turn off the flame by closing the _____ valve on the torch first. Then close the _____ valve on the torch.

AIRCRAFT WELDING

17. Low _____, low _____ steels are the ferrous materials that are gas welded most frequently.

18. As in aluminum welding, _____ is needed to break down surface oxides and ensure a sound weld.

19. The principle use of _____ solder in aircraft work is in the fabrication process of high pressure _____ lines.

20. The heat control of a TIG welder may be preset by a machine setting or variable by use of a _____ or a _____ control.

21. The grinding of a Tungsten electrode used in TIG welding should be done _____, not _____.

22. When welding aluminum the welding machine is set to an _____ output waveform because it causes a _____ that breaks up _____.

23. A good indication and measure of weld quality for titanium is the weld _____. A bright _____ weld indicates that the shielding is satisfactory.

24. What four types of welds are commonly used in flat position welding?

    1. _____   3. _____

    2. _____   4. _____

25. Stresses developed by heating and cooling during welding need to be relieved or _____ and _____ of the sheets will occur.

26. If a partial replacement of a tube is necessary, make an _____ sleeve splice, especially where you want a smooth tube surface.

27. Dents at a cluster weld can be repaired by welding a _____ over the dented area.

28. A damaged tubular section can be repaired using welded _____ reinforcements.

29. The spring-steel part of a spring-steel leave is _____ and should not be _____ on.

30. The preferred method to repair an engine mount member is by using a _____ replacement tube.

AIRCRAFT WELDING

Section A
True of False

_____ 1. Friction stir welding is one of the most common welding techniques.

_____ 2. Gas welding was the most common welding method for thick (over 3/16") till the 1950s.

_____ 3. The temperature generated by SMAW is hotter than gas welding.

_____ 4. GMAW (MIG) welding is an improvement over SMAW (stick) welding.

_____ 5. GTAW (TIG) uses a consumable rod and a filler.

_____ 6. Plasma cutting systems can cut aluminum and stainless steel.

_____ 7. The acetylene pressure gauge should never be set higher than 20 psi for welding or cutting.

_____ 8. The acetylene hose is red and has left hand threads.

_____ 9. The flash back arrestor prevents the reverse flow of gas.

_____ 10. A backfire is a momentary backward flow of the gases at the torch tip.

_____ 11. Welding eyewear used for gas welding can also be used for arc welding processes.

_____ 12. Welding tips have a number of holes and cutting tips have one hole.

_____ 13. Open the torch oxygen valve a quarter to a half turn when lightening the torch.

_____ 14. The neutral flame burns higher than the carburizing flame.

_____ 15. When shutting down the welding equipment the oxygen valve is closed first.

_____ 16. For welding thick metals or heavy plate, a technique called backhand welding can be used.

_____ 17. Maintain a slight excess of acetylene for most steels, and a neutral flame for stainless

_____ 18. Gas welding of some aluminum alloys can be accomplished successfully.

_____ 19. Welding magnesium is done with a slightly carburizing flame.

_____ 20. Pure tungsten electrodes have better electron emission characteristics than Thoriated electrodes.

_____ 21. When TIG welding aluminum the welding equipment is switched to a AC output waveform.

_____ 22. TIG welding of titanium is performed using AC straight polarity.

_____ 23. Expansion and contraction caused by heat during the welding process have a tendency to buckle and warp thin sheet metal sheets.

_____ 24. Tack welding at intervals of the joint could control the expansion of the sheets that are welded.

_____ 25. A damaged tubular section can be repaired using a formed steel patch plate.

Chapter 5, Section A - Aircraft Welding

Name: _____ Date: _____

AIRCRAFT WELDING

PAGE LEFT BLANK INTENTIONALLY

AIRCRAFT WELDING

Section B
Knowledge Application Questions

1. What is the preferred method of welding magnesium?

2. What is a safety hazard associated with welding magnesium?

3. What must be done in the weld zone to successfully weld titanium?

4. Why is it necessary to use flux in all silver soldering?

5. What type of flame is used for silver soldering?

6. What type of repair could be made for a dented steel tube cluster joint?

7. What method can be used to insert a tight fitting inner sleeve into a tubular repair?

8. How is a soft flame obtained without reducing thermal output?

9. What is the most extensively used method of welding aluminum?

AIRCRAFT WELDING

10. What valve should be turned off first when extinguishing a torch?

11. What procedure will control expansion when welding a joint?

12. What safety precaution should be taken when gas welding has been completed?

13. What must be done with heat-treated aluminum alloys after a welding repair has been made?

14. What is the result of insufficient penetration?

15. What type of welding causes less buckling and warping than gas welding?

16. What is gas shielded arc welding?

17. What are some advantages of gas shielded arc welding?

18. What are three general types of welding?

19. What does the size of the torch tip opening determine?

AIRCRAFT WELDING

20. What three types of flames can be adjusted during Oxyacetylene welding?

21. What type of steel is commonly used for tubular steel structures in aircraft?

22. What principal factor governs the size of a welding tip?

23. When welding a structure that will require heat-treating, what type of filler rod must be used?

24. When welding a section of tubing into a structure, why is it a good practice to allow one end to

25. At what angle is the scarf for a repair sleeve cut?

26. Describe a fishmouth cut for a sleeve.

27. Why is a fishmouth joint stronger than a scarf joint?

28. Describe a rosette weld.

29. Explain how a fuselage structure can be held in alignment while making welded repairs.

AIRCRAFT WELDING

30. What precaution must be taken before welding fuel and oil tanks?

AIRCRAFT WELDING

Section C
Final Chapter Exam

1. Edge notching is generally recommended in butt welding above a certain thickness of aluminum because its _____
   - ☐ A. helps hold the metal in alignment during welding.
   - ☐ B. aids in the removal or penetration of oxides on the metal surface.
   - ☐ C. aids in getting full penetration of the metal and prevents local distortion.

2. Where should the flux be applied when oxyacetylene welding aluminum?
   - ☐ A. Painted only on the surface to be welded.
   - ☐ B. Painted on the surface to be welded and applied to the welding rod.
   - ☐ C. Applied only to the welding rod.

3. What purpose does flux serve in welding aluminum?
   - ☐ A. Removes dirt, grease, and oil.
   - ☐ B. Minimizes or prevents oxidation.
   - ☐ C. Ensures proper distribution of the filler rod.

4. Why are aluminum plates 1/4-inch or more thick usually preheated before welding?
   - ☐ A. Reduces internal stresses and assures more complete penetration.
   - ☐ B. Reduces welding time.
   - ☐ C. Prevents corrosion and ensures proper distribution of flux.

5. How should a welding torch flame be adjusted to weld stainless steel?
   - ☐ A. Slightly carburizing.
   - ☐ B. Slightly oxidizing.
   - ☐ C. Neutral.

6. Oxides form rapidly when alloys or metals are hot. So it is important when welding aluminum to use a _____
   - ☐ A. solvent.
   - ☐ B. filler.
   - ☐ C. flux.

7. In gas welding, the amount of heat applied to the material being welded is controlled by the _____
   - ☐ A. amount of gas pressure used.
   - ☐ B. size of the tip opening.
   - ☐ C. distance the tip is held from the work.

8. The shielding gases generally used in the Gas Tungsten Arc (GTA) welding of aluminum consist of _____
   - ☐ A. a mixture of nitrogen and carbon dioxide.
   - ☐ B. nitrogen or hydrogen, or a mixture of nitrogen and hydrogen.
   - ☐ C. helium or argon, or a mixture of helium and argon.

9. Acetylene at a line pressure above 15 PSI is _____
   - ☐ A. dangerously unstable.
   - ☐ B. used when a reducing flame is necessary.
   - ☐ C. usually necessary when welding metal over 3/8-inch thick.

10. If too much acetylene is used in the welding of stainless steel _____
    - ☐ A. a porous weld will result.
    - ☐ B. the metal will absorb carbon and lose its resistance to corrosion.
    - ☐ C. oxide will be formed on the base metal close to the weld.

AIRCRAFT WELDING

11. In Gas Tungsten Arc (GTA) welding, a stream of inert gas is used to _____
    - ☐ A. prevent the formation of oxides in the puddle.
    - ☐ B. concentrate the heat of the arc and prevent its dissipation.
    - ☐ C. lower the temperature required to properly fuse the metal.

12. When a butt welded joint is visually inspected for penetration _____
    - ☐ A. the penetration should be 25 to 50 percent of the thickness of the base metal.
    - ☐ B. the penetration should be 100 percent of the thickness of the base metal.
    - ☐ C. look for evidence of excessive heat in the form of a very high bead.

13. Why is it necessary to use flux in all silver soldering operations?
    - ☐ A. To chemically clean the base metal of oxide film.
    - ☐ B. To prevent overheating of the base metal.
    - ☐ C. To increase heat conductivity.

14. A welding torch backfire may be caused by _____
    - ☐ A. a loose tip.
    - ☐ B. using too much acetylene.
    - ☐ C. a tip temperature that is too cool.

15. Which statement best describes magnesium welding?
    - ☐ A. Magnesium can be welded to other metals.
    - ☐ B. Filler rod should be nickel steel.
    - ☐ C. Filler rod should be the same composition as base metal.

16. Welding over brazed or soldered joints is _____
    - ☐ A. not permitted.
    - ☐ B. permissible for mild steel.
    - ☐ C. permissible for most metals or alloys that are not heat treated.

17. In selecting a torch tip size to use in welding, the size of the tip opening determines the _____
    - ☐ A. amount of heat applied to the work.
    - ☐ B. temperature of the flame.
    - ☐ C. melting point of the filler metal.

18. Why should a carburizing flame be avoided when welding steel?
    - ☐ A. It removes the carbon content.
    - ☐ B. It hardens the surface.
    - ☐ C. A cold weld will result.

19. The most important consideration(s) when selecting welding rod is _____
    - ☐ A. current setting or flame temperature.
    - ☐ B. material compatibility.
    - ☐ C. ambient conditions.

20. Which statement is true in regard to welding heat-treated magnesium?
    - ☐ A. The welded section does not have the strength of the original metal.
    - ☐ B. Flux should not be used because it is very difficult to remove and is likely to cause corrosion.
    - ☐ C. Magnesium cannot be repaired by fusion welding because of the high probability of igniting the metal.

21. The use of electric-arc welding techniques on ferrous metals may result in the metal becoming magnetized. Magnetism should be removed by _____
    - ☐ A. striking the welded area with a hammer no less than six blows.
    - ☐ B. zinc-chromating the welded area.
    - ☐ C. the use of a degausser.

22. When designing a welded patch repair the patch should extend _____
    - ☐ A. to a length equal to the damaged area.
    - ☐ B. 1 inch beyond each end of the damaged area.
    - ☐ C. 1.5 times the diameter of the damaged tube beyond the damaged area.

23. When cutting an angle for splice welds, the angle should be _____
    - ☐ A. 15°.
    - ☐ B. 30°.
    - ☐ C. 45°.

24. The purpose of a rosette weld is to _____
    - ☐ A. allow a means of transmitting loads between structural members.
    - ☐ B. ease the stress buildup during the expansion experienced during welding.
    - ☐ C. maintain the relative positions of the tubes.

25. Exhaust system components should be welded using _____
    - ☐ A. oxyacetylene.
    - ☐ B. electric arc.
    - ☐ C. a form of inert-gas welding.

Chapter 5, Final Chapter Exam - Aircraft Welding

Name: _____ Date: _____

AIRCRAFT WELDING

PAGE LEFT BLANK INTENTIONALLY

AIRCRAFT WOOD AND STRUCTURAL REPAIR

CHAPTER 6

Section A
Study Aid Questions - Fill In The Blanks

1. The ideal range of moisture content in a wood aircraft structure is _____ percent, with any readings over _____ percent providing an environment for the growth of fungus in the wood.

2. A good indication of moisture, fungal growth, and possible _____ is a _____ or _____ odor.

3. Aircraft that are exposed to large cyclic changes of _____ and _____ are especially prone to wood shrinkage that may lead to glue joint _____ .

4. Glued joints are generally designed to take _____ loads.

5. Wood _____ and dry _____ are usually easy to detect. _____ may be evident as either a discoloration or a softening of the wood.

6. Dark discoloration or gray stains running along the grain are indicative of _____ .

7. Inspect structural members for _____ failures, which is indicated by rupture across the wood fibers.

8. Tapping a wood structure with a light plastic hammer should produce a _____ sound.

9. _____ is the preferred choice of wood and the standard by which the other wood types are measured.

10. All solid wood and _____ should be of the highest quality and grade.

11. All woods used for structural repair of aircraft are classified as _____ .

12. Pin knot clusters are acceptable if they produce only a small effect on _____ .

13. _____ are acceptable if careful inspection fails to reveal any decay.

AIRCRAFT WOOD AND STRUCTURAL REPAIR

14. Checks are longitudinal _____, in general extending across the annual rings.

15. _____ wood is characterized by high specific gravity.

16. Some of the more common adhesives that have been used in aircraft construction and repair include _____, _____, _____ and, _____ adhesives.

17. _____ are a useful means of detecting the presence of wax on a wood surface or joint.

18. Satisfactory glue joints in aircraft should develop the _____ of the wood under all conditions of _____.

19. _____ are the most satisfactory method of fabricating an end joint between two solid members.

20. A damaged spar may be spliced at almost any point except at _____, _____, _____, or lift and interplane strut fittings.

Section A
True of False

_____ 1. A certificated mechanic who has not performed repairs to wooden aircraft previously, is not allowed to perform repairs to a wood aircraft structure.

_____ 2. When inspecting an aircraft constructed or comprised of wood components the moisture content must be above 20%.

_____ 3. Some slight sectional undulation or bulging between panels of aircraft using single plywood covering may be permissible if the wood and glue are sound.

_____ 4. Glued joints are generally designed to take bearing loads.

_____ 5. Dark discoloration of wood or gray stains running along the grain are indicative of water penetration.

_____ 6. The condition of the fabric covering on plywood surfaces does not provide a useful indication of the condition of the wood underneath.

_____ 7. Compression failures are indicated by rupture across the wood fibers.

_____ 8. When during an inspection of a wood structure a soft and mushy area is found, the mechanic should disassemble and repair that structure.

_____ 9. Douglas fir is the preferred choice of wood and the standard by which other woods are measured.

_____ 10. All woods used for structural repair of aircraft are classifies as hardwoods.

_____ 11. Wavy, curly, interlocked grain are acceptable, if local irregularities do not exceed limitations specified for spiral and diagonal grain.

AIRCRAFT WOOD AND STRUCTURAL REPAIR

True of False (continued)

_____ 12. Hard knots are not acceptable in wood species used for aircraft repair.

_____ 13. Checks, shakes, and splits are acceptable under certain conditions in wood repair.

_____ 14. Decay on aircraft wooden parts for repair are never acceptable.

_____ 15. Smooth even surfaces produced on planers and joiners with sharp knives and correct feed adjustments are the best surfaces for gluing solid wood.

_____ 16. The proper way to prepare wood surfaces is to sand the surface with a 180 grit sandpaper.

_____ 17. All gluing operations should be performed above 70°F for proper performance of the adhesive.

_____ 18. The repairs to solid or laminated spars are never permitted and the spar should be replaced with a new spar from the manufacturer or the holder of a PMA for that part.

_____ 19. A fabric patch could be used to repair holes not exceeding 1 inch in diameter.

_____ 20. A properly prepared and installed scarf patch is the bests repair for damaged plywood and is preferred for most skin repairs.

Chapter 6, Section A - Aircraft Wood and Structural Repair

Name:_____   Date:_____

AIRCRAFT WOOD AND STRUCTURAL REPAIR

PAGE LEFT BLANK INTENTIONALLY

AIRCRAFT WOOD AND STRUCTURAL REPAIR

Section B
Knowledge Application Questions

1. Describe what a laminated wood assembly consists of?

2. How is aircraft plywood different from laminated wood?

3. What species of wood is used as a standard for strength properties?

4. How can rot be revealed during an inspection of a wood structure?

5. What types of glues are used in aircraft wood structure repair?

6. What effects do room temperature have on gluing wood structures using resin glue or epoxy adhesives?

7. Under what condition are mineral streaks acceptable?

8. Are hard knots acceptable in aircraft quality wood?

9. Explain why compressed wood is not acceptable for aircraft wood structures?

10. Why is it necessary to examine all stains and discoloration carefully?

11. Why are light steel bushings sometimes used in wooden structures?

AIRCRAFT WOOD AND STRUCTURAL REPAIR

12. What are the results of non-uniform gluing pressure?

13. Name 3 methods that are used to apply pressure to wood glue joints?

    1.

    2.

    3.

14. What is the most effective type of joint used in splicing structural members?

15. Why does the strength of a beveled scarf joint depend on the accuracy of the beveled cut?

16. Always splice and reinforce plywood webs with what type of wood?

17. What method will prevent a patch and a plywood pressure plate from adhering together due to extruding glue from the patch?

18. What areas of a wood spar may not be spliced?

19. Why are bushings made of plastic or light metal used on wooden structures?

20. What is the minimum temperature for curing wood joints with resin glue or epoxy adhesives?

Chapter 6, Section B - Aircraft Wood and Structural Repair

Name:_____   Date:_____

AIRCRAFT WOOD AND STRUCTURAL REPAIR

Section C
Final Chapter Exam

1. Which statement about wood decay is correct?
   - ☐ A. Decay that occurs before the wood is seasoned does not affect the strength of the finished piece.
   - ☐ B. A limited amount of certain kinds of decay is acceptable in aircraft woods since decay affects the binding between the fibers and not the fibers themselves.
   - ☐ C. Decay is not acceptable in any form or amount.

2. Compression failures in wood aircraft structures are characterized by buckling of the fibers that appear as streaks on the surface _____
   - ☐ A. at right angles to the growth rings.
   - ☐ B. parallel to the grain.
   - ☐ C. at right angles to the grain.

3. Glue deterioration in wood aircraft structure is indicated _____
   - ☐ A. when a joint has separated and the glue surface shows only the imprint of the wood with no wood fibers clinging to the glue.
   - ☐ B. when a joint has separated and the glue surface shows pieces of wood or wood fibers clinging to the glue.
   - ☐ C. by any joint separation.

4. When patching a plywood skin, abrupt changes in cross sectional areas which will develop dangerous stress concentration should be avoided by using _____
   - ☐ A. circular or elliptical patches.
   - ☐ B. square patches.
   - ☐ C. doublers with any desired shaped patches.

5. Laminated wood is sometimes used in the construction of highly stressed aircraft components. This wood can be identified by its _____
   - ☐ A. parallel grain construction.
   - ☐ B. similarity to standard plywood construction.
   - ☐ C. perpendicular grain construction.

6. Pin knot clusters are permitted in wood aircraft structure provided _____
   - ☐ A. they produce a small effect on grain direction.
   - ☐ B. they have no mineral streaks.
   - ☐ C. no pitch pockets are within 12".

7. Which of the following conditions will determine acceptance of wood with mineral streaks?
   - ☐ A. Careful inspection fails to reveal any decay.
   - ☐ B. They produce only a small effect on grain direction.
   - ☐ C. Local irregularities do not exceed limitations specified for spiral and diagonal grain.

8. A faint line running across the grain of a wood spar generally indicates _____
   - ☐ A. compression failure.
   - ☐ B. shear failure.
   - ☐ C. decay.

9. In cases of elongated bolt holes in a wood spar, or cracks in the vicinity of bolt holes _____
   - ☐ A. it is permissible to ream the hole, plug with hardwood, and redrill.
   - ☐ B. the spar may be reinforced by using hardwood reinforcing plates.
   - ☐ C. a new section of spar should be spliced in or the spar replaced entirely.

10. Where is information found concerning acceptable species substitutions for wood materials used in aircraft repair?
    - ☐ A. Aircraft Specifications or Type Certificate Data Sheets.
    - ☐ B. Technical Standard Orders.
    - ☐ C. AC 43.13-1B.

AIRCRAFT WOOD AND STRUCTURAL REPAIR

11. The strength of a well designed and properly prepared wood splice joint is provided by the _____
    - ☐ A. bearing surface of the wood fibers.
    - ☐ B. glue.
    - ☐ C. reinforcement plates.

12. Why is the I-beam wooden spar routed?
    - ☐ A. To increase strength.
    - ☐ B. To obtain uniform strength.
    - ☐ C. To reduce weight.

13. Laminated wood spars may be substituted for solid rectangular wood spars _____
    - ☐ A. only if the strength deficiency is allowed for by an increase in dimension.
    - ☐ B. if the same quality wood is used in both.
    - ☐ C. only upon specific approval by the manufacturer or the FAA.

14. For what reason are sodium salts and lime added to Casein glue?
    - ☐ A. to prevent cracking of the glue after it has cured
    - ☐ B. To prevent attack by microorganisms.
    - ☐ C. In order for paint to adhere to it.

15. Which type of wood is considered standard for aircraft constructions, and of which all other types of wood are compared?
    - ☐ A. Douglas Fir.
    - ☐ B. Hemlock.
    - ☐ C. Spruce.

16. Compression failures in wood structures are characterized by buckling of the fibers that appear as streaks on the surface _____
    - ☐ A. at right angles to the growth rings.
    - ☐ B. only in the spring wood or summer wood.
    - ☐ C. at right angles to the grain.

17. Wood spars must be _____
    - ☐ A. of solid construction.
    - ☐ B. may not be drilled.
    - ☐ C. may be of laminated construction.

18. Wood spars may _____
    - ☐ A. not be repaired.
    - ☐ B. be repaired only once, assuming there is not question of integrity.
    - ☐ C. be repaired twice, assuming there is not a question of integrity.

19. In order to properly inspect a laminated wood spar, _____
    - ☐ A. all gussets must be removed.
    - ☐ B. all bolts should be loosened.
    - ☐ C. all ribs must be removed.

20. The moisture content of wood at the time of gluing should be in the range of _____
    - ☐ A. 0-4 percent.
    - ☐ B. 5-8 percent.
    - ☐ C. 8-12 percent.

Chapter 6, Final Chapter Exam - Aircraft Wood and Structural Repair

Name: _____   Date: _____

ADVANCED COMPOSITE MATERIALS

CHAPTER 7

Section A
Study Aid Questions - Fill In The Blanks

1. What are the three primary advantages of composite materials?

    1.   2.   3.

2. Name five applications of composites on aircraft.

    1.   3.   5.

    2.   4.

3. List the two major components of a laminate.

    1.   2.

4. List four examples of honey comb structures on aircraft.

    1.   3.

    2.   4.

5. List four advantages of Thermoplastic honeycomb material.

    1.   3.

    2.   4.

6. What are two advantages to using Polystyrene in sandwich structures?

    1.   2.

7. List four composite manufacturing defects.

    1.   3.

    2.   4.

ADVANCED COMPOSITE MATERIALS

8. List four sources of composite manufacturing defects.

   1.   3.

   2.   4.

9. Matrix cracks, or micro cracks, can significantly reduce properties dependant on the resin or the fiber/resin interface, such as _____ and _____.

10. List three types of damage to the composite surface that is detectable via a visual inspection.

    1.   2.   3.

11. List four types of discrepancies that can be detected with a visual inspection.

    1.   3.

    2.   4.

12. The signal from an unflawed region is used for _____, and any deviation from this unflawed signal (period) indicates the existence of _____.

13. List four contaminants that prepreg materials must be protected from.

    1.   3.

    2.   4.

14. _____ utilizes precured composite detail parts, and uses a layer of adhesive to bond two procured composite parts.

15. Precured laminates undergoing secondary bonding usually have a thin _____ or _____ peel ply cured onto the bonding surface.

16. List three advantages of using composite doublers to repair metal skin components.

    1.   2.   3.

ADVANCED COMPOSITE MATERIALS

17. List the four types of bleed out techniques.

    1.   3.

    2.   4.

18. A temporary repair must meet the _____ but is limited by time or flight cycles.

19. A _____ repair can be used to repair damage to a sandwich honeycomb structure.

20. Water in the honeycomb core could _____ at high altitudes.

21. Sold laminate structures have _____ plies than the face sheets of honeycomb structures.

22. Resin injection repairs are used on _____ structures for _____ damages to a solid laminate.

23. Aircraft radomes are made of _____ material.

24. The properties of a _____ repair are not as good as a repair with _____ material, but by using a _____ method the properties of a _____ can be improved.

25. The disadvantage of bonded repairs is that most repair materials require _____, and _____ procedures.

26. Bolted repairs are not desirable for _____ structure due to the thin face sheets that have limited _____ strength.

27. Most composite primary structures for the aircraft industry are fastened with _____ or _____ fasteners

28. Drill bits used for carbon fiber and fiber glass are made from _____ material or _____ because the fibers are so hard that _____ drill bits will not last very long.

29. Countersinking a composite structure is required when _____ fasteners are used.

30. Drilling in composite material require _____ speeds and _____ feeds than drilling in metallic structures.

Chapter 7, Section A - Advanced Composite Materials

Name:_____   Date:_____

ADVANCED COMPOSITE MATERIALS

PAGE LEFT BLANK INTENTIONALLY

ADVANCED COMPOSITE MATERIALS

Section B
Knowledge Application Questions

1. Describe the term Homogeneous as it applies to laminate structures.

2. Describe the term Anisotropic as it applies to laminate structures.

3. Describe the term Quasi-isotropic as it applies to laminate structures.

4. What benefit do most fabric constructions offer that straight unidirectional tapes do not?

5. What is a benefit of tightly woven fabrics on aerospace structures?

6. Name one type of conductive material used to protect composite components against lightening strikes?

7. Why are Phenolic resins used for interior components?

8. How many stages are there to curing resins and what are they?

9. Briefly explain why prepreg materials must be kept in a freezer at zero degrees Fahrenheit.

ADVANCED COMPOSITE MATERIALS

10. Bell shaped core cells, or flexicore, is used for what applications?

11. Explain what the benefits are for using honeycomb with a high density and small core cells.

12. Describe what it means for a part to be resin rich.

13. Describe what it means for a part to be resin starved.

14. Briefly explain the Audible Sonic Testing method.

15. Describe the sound indicative of a well-bonded solid structure when utilizing the Audible Sonic Testing method.

16. Describe the sound indicative of a discrepant area when utilizing the Audible Sonic Testing Method.

17. Describe what could produce a faulty result when utilizing the Audible sonic test.

18. Briefly describe how the Through Transmission Ultrasonic inspection method works.

19. If a clean room is not available for prepreg material layup, what techniques are used to prevent contamination?

ADVANCED COMPOSITE MATERIALS

20. What is co-curing and describe a typical co-cure application?

21. What is the difference between a permanent repair and an interim repair?

22. What is the restriction of potted repair related to flight controls?

23. Why does water/moisture needs to be removed before a repair to a honeycomb part is cured?

24. Explain the resin injection repair method.

25. Describe why aircraft radomes need to be made of only 3 or 4 plies of fiberglass.

26. What is the typical fiber orientation of a quasi-isotropic lay up?

27. Explain the difference between laminate symmetry and laminate balance.

28. What are the three most common fiber materials used for aerospace structures?

29. Explain why lightning protection fibers and materials are necessary for composite aircraft.

ADVANCED COMPOSITE MATERIALS

30. Explain briefly what thermoplastic resin systems are and how they differ from thermosetting resin systems.

Chapter 7, Section B - Advanced Composite Materials

Name:_____ Date:_____

ADVANCED COMPOSITE MATERIALS

Section C
Final Chapter Exam

1. What is the role of the Matrix component in the composite material?
   - ☐ A. The Matrix is the primary load carrying element.
   - ☐ B. The Matrix supports the fibers and bonds them together.
   - ☐ C. The Matrix determines the direction that the composite material will be strongest.

2. What do the structural properties such as stiffness, dimensional stability, and strength of a composite laminate depend on?
   - ☐ A. The curing temperature.
   - ☐ B. The size of the fibers.
   - ☐ C. The stacking sequence of the plies.

3. In this ply orientation, the plies are stacked in a 0, -45, 45 and 90 degrees sequence or in a 0,-60 and +60 degree sequences. These types of ply orientation simulate the properties of a/an _____ material.
   - ☐ A. Bi-directional.
   - ☐ B. Quasi-isotropic.
   - ☐ C. Isotropic.

4. Unidirectional tape products have which of the following physical properties?
   - ☐ A. High shear strength perpendicular to the fiber direction.
   - ☐ B. High compressive strength across the fibers.
   - ☐ C. High tensile strength in the fiber direction.

5. Kevlar® is DuPont®'s trademark name for what type of fibers?
   - ☐ A. Thermoplastics.
   - ☐ B. Polyester.
   - ☐ D. Aramid.

6. What is the primary advantage of Aramid fibers?
   - ☐ A. Resistant to impact damage.
   - ☐ B. Flexibility.
   - ☐ C. Hygroscopic..

7. If the graphene layers or planes stack with a two dimensional order, the material is defined as _____
   - ☐ A. carbon.
   - ☐ B. graphite.
   - ☐ C. aramid.

8. What is required for aircraft carbon fiber parts that are prone to lightening strike?
   - ☐ A. Strapping to non-conductive aircraft parts.
   - ☐ B. Alternating aluminum plies.
   - ☐ C. Lightening protection.

9. What are Ceramic fibers used for on aircraft?
   - ☐ A. Turbine blades.
   - ☐ B. Turbine blades.
   - ☐ C. Exhaust Nozzles.

10. Where are Bismaleimide (BMI) resins used?
    - ☐ A. Cabin interiors.
    - ☐ B. High temperature components.
    - ☐ C. Control surfaces.

11. Most honeycomb materials are _____; that is, properties are directional.
    - ☐ A. anisotropic
    - ☐ B. isotropic
    - ☐ C. quasi-isotropic

ADVANCED COMPOSITE MATERIALS

12. Honeycomb core cells for aerospace applications are typically what shape?
    - ☐ A. Pentagons.
    - ☐ B. Octagons.
    - ☐ C. Hexagons.

13. What is considered to be the optimal fiber to resin ratio?
    - ☐ A. 40:60
    - ☐ B. 60:40
    - ☐ C. 70:30

14. What causes delaminations to form?
    - ☐ A. Matrix cracks.
    - ☐ B. Overheating.
    - ☐ C. Tension loads.

15. What type of inspection is the primary method for in-service inspections of composite materials?
    - ☐ A. Audible Sonic Testing.
    - ☐ B. Visual.
    - ☐ C. Ultrasonic.

16. On what type of composite structures is tap testing most effective?
    - ☐ A. Thick skin panels.
    - ☐ B. Honeycomb sandwich with thin face sheets.
    - ☐ C. Isotropic face sheets.

17. What Ultrasonic Inspection method uses two transducers, one on each side of the area to be inspected?
    - ☐ A. Through transmission.
    - ☐ B. Pulse echo.
    - ☐ C. Ultrasonic bond tester.

18. What Ultrasonic Inspection method uses a single search unit as a transmitting and receiving transducer that is excited by high voltage pulses?
    - ☐ A. Through transmission.
    - ☐ B. Pulse echo.
    - ☐ C. Ultrasonic bond tester.

19. What type of inspection is the primary method for in-service inspections of composite materials?
    - ☐ A. Visual.
    - ☐ B. Automated tap testing.
    - ☐ C. Ultrasonic.

20. What is the typical storage life for prepreg material?
    - ☐ A. 2 to 8 months.
    - ☐ B. 4 to 10 months.
    - ☐ C. 6 to 12 months.

21. What is used to improve the peel strength of co-bonded assemblies?
    - ☐ A. Film adhesive.
    - ☐ B. Silicon adhesive.
    - ☐ C. Enhanced epoxy resin.

22. What is considered to be a permanent repair?
    - ☐ A. Meet the strength requirements but is limited by time of flight cycles.
    - ☐ B. Meet the strength requirements but has a different inspection schedule.
    - ☐ C. Meet the strength requirements and the durability requirements.

23. A potted repair is for _____
    - ☐ A. small repairs to flight controls.
    - ☐ B. large repairs to honeycomb engine cowlings.
    - ☐ C. small repairs to honeycomb structure.

24. What condition could affect the signal of the aircraft radar?
    - ☐ A. Trapped water in the aircraft radome.
    - ☐ B. Scarved repairs made to the radome.
    - ☐ C. Large potted repairs made to the radome.

25. Honeycomb sandwich structures are often repaired with _____
    - ☐ A. scarf type bonded repair.
    - ☐ B. scarf type bolted repair.
    - ☐ C. an external bolted repair.

Chapter 7, Final Chapter Exam - Advanced Composite Materials

Name:_____   Date:_____

ADVANCED COMPOSITE MATERIALS

AIRCRAFT PAINTING AND FINISHING

CHAPTER 8

Section A
Study Aid Questions - Fill In The Blanks

1. Paint is more than aesthetics, it affects the _____ of the aircraft and protects the _____ of the airframe.

2. _____ is at the top of the list when compared to other coatings for abrasion, stain, and chemical resistant properties.

3. There are several methods of applying aircraft finish. Among the most common are: _____ _____, and _____.

4. There are two main types of spray equipment: _____ and _____.

5. The three most common types of spray guns used are: _____, and _____.

6. The HVLP production spray gun is an _____ mix gun. The _____ and _____ is mixed inside the air cap.

7. The most important part of any painting project is the _____.

8. The _____ control knob of a spray gun controls the airflow (pattern shape)

9. Primer is typically applied using a _____ spray pattern.

10. While painting the second pass will overlap the first pass by _____ percent.

11. A quick check of the spray pattern can be verified by spraying some _____ or _____ through the gun.

12. A pulsating, or spitting fan pattern may be caused by a _____, _____ vent hole on the supply cup, or the _____ may be leaking around the needle.

13. Blushing is the dull _____ that appears in a paint finish.

AIRCRAFT PAINTING AND FINISHING

14. Pin holes are the result of _____, _____ or _____.

15. Sags and runs are caused by applying _____ paint to an area, by holding the spray gun _____ to the surface, or moving the gun _____ across the surface.

16. Orange peel refers to the appearance of a _____ surface.

17. Fisheyes appear as _____ in the coating as it is being applied.

18. Wrinkling is usually caused by _____ and _____ of the paint finish due to excessively thick or solvent heavy paint coats.

19. Spray dust could be caused by spray gun held _____ from the surface, or incorrect spray gun _____.

20. For a spot repair that requires blending of the coating, an area about _____ times the area of the actual repair must be prepared.

Section A
True of False

_____ 1. The top coat applied to external parts of the aircraft protect against corrosion and deterioration.

_____ 2. Epoxy primer is recommended for steel tube frame aircraft prior to installing fabric covering.

_____ 3. Older type zinc chromate primers are distinguishable by their flat green color.

_____ 4. If the paint materials are too thick, they are likely to run or not cover the surface adequately.

_____ 5. An HVLP spray gun transfers more paint to the surface of the painted surface.

_____ 6. The HVLP spray gun is an external mix gun.

_____ 7. Fresh air breathing systems should be used when spraying polyurethane paint because it contains isocyanides.

_____ 8. The Zahn cup is used to measure the viscosity of the primer or paint system.

_____ 9. Alodine is not used with aluminum aircraft, it is mostly used with composite aircraft structures.

_____ 10. The upper control knob of the paint gun controls the airflow and the bottom control knob controls the fluid flow.

_____ 11. If the spray pattern is offset to one side or the other, the fluid valve may be plugged.

_____ 12. A spitting fan pattern may be caused by a loose nozzle, clogged vent hole or a leaking packing.

AIRCRAFT PAINTING AND FINISHING

True of False (continued)

_____ 13. When painting an aircraft, start painting the large surfaces first and than fill in the corners and gaps.

_____ 14. Blushing is the dull milky haze that appears in a paint finish.

_____ 15. Orange peel could be caused by not enough reducer or too little flash time between coats.

_____ 16. The most effective way to eliminate fisheyes is to ensure that the temperature is above 70°F.

_____ 17. Each operator of an aircraft shall display on the aircraft, marks consisting of the Roman capital letter "U" (denoting United States registration).

_____ 18. The registration marks must be at least 10 inches high. A glider may display marks at least 3 inches.

_____ 19. One way to test if paint is old is to apply turbine oil to a small area. If the paint softens within a few minutes the paint system is an acrylic or epoxy paint finish.

_____ 20. Plastic Media Blasting (PMB) is an effective way of stripping paint of composite structures which causes less damage than sanding.

Chapter 8, Section A - Aircraft Painting and Finishing

AIRCRAFT PAINTING AND FINISHING

PAGE LEFT BLANK INTENTIONALLY

AIRCRAFT PAINTING AND FINISHING

Section B
Knowledge Application Questions

1. What are the common types of paint used on aircraft?

2. Why are old zinc type primers (bright yellow color) not used anymore for modern aircraft.

3. What will happen if the ports in the horn of the spray gun aircap are becoming plugged?

4. What is the purpose of primers?

5. Many of the solvents and thinners used in modern finishing systems are toxic; what health safety precautions should the mechanic observe?

6. What are three methods of applying paint?

    1.   2.   3.

7. What is the cause of spray dust?

8. What may cause spray paint sags and runs?

9. What causes orange peel spray mottle?

10. What is a blushing paint finish?

11. What will cause a blushing paint finish?

AIRCRAFT PAINTING AND FINISHING

12. What could be the result of applying a coat of paint when the temperature of the dope room is too high?

13. What areas must be protected from damage when using paint remover/stripper?

14. What is the reason for paint touchup other than appearance?

15. What is the most common finish system for modern transport category aircraft?

16. Name three ways to strip paint from an aircraft.

    1.   2.   3.

17. Describe how to adjust a spray gun for painting large surfaces.

18. What could cause a pulsating or spitting fan pattern?

19. What is the most effective way to eliminate fisheyes?

20. What is the location of the registration mark on fixed wing aircraft?

Chapter 8, Section B - Aircraft Painting and Finishing

Name:_____   Date:_____

AIRCRAFT PAINTING AND FINISHING

Section C
Final Chapter Exam

1. Which of the following is a hazard associated with sanding on fabric surfaces during the finishing process?
   - ☐ A. Overheating of the fabric/finish, especially with the use of power tools.
   - ☐ B. Static electricity buildup.
   - ☐ C. Embedding of particles in the finish.

2. What is likely to occur if unhydrated wash primer is applied to unpainted aluminum and then about 30 to 40 minutes later a finish topcoat, when the humidity is low?
   - ☐ A. Corrosion.
   - ☐ B. A glossy, blush-free finish.
   - ☐ C. A dull finish due to the topcoat 'sinking in' to primer that is still too soft.

3. Before applying a protective coating to any unpainted clean aluminum, you should _____
   - ☐ A. wipe the surface with avgas or kerosene.
   - ☐ B. remove any conversion coating film.
   - ☐ C. avoid touching the surface with bare hands.

4. What is the usual cause of runs and sags in aircraft finishes?
   - ☐ A. Too much material applied in one coat.
   - ☐ B. Material is being applied too fast.
   - ☐ C. Low atmospheric humidity.

5. Which defect in aircraft finishes may be caused by adverse humidity, drafts, or sudden changes in temperature?
   - ☐ A. Orange peel.
   - ☐ B. Blushing.
   - ☐ C. Pinholes.

6. If masking tape is left on for several days and/or exposed to heat, it is likely that the tape will _____
   - ☐ A. not seal out the finishing material if the delay or heating occurs before spraying.
   - ☐ B. be weakened in its ability to adhere to the surface.
   - ☐ C. cure to the finish and be very difficult to remove.

7. What is used to slow the drying time of some finishes and to prevent blush?
   - ☐ A. Reducer.
   - ☐ B. Retarder.
   - ☐ C. Rejuvenator.

8. Which type of coating typically includes phosphoric acid as one of its components at the time of application?
   - ☐ A. Wash primer.
   - ☐ B. Epoxy primer.
   - ☐ C. Zinc chromate primer.

9. Which properly applied finish topcoat is the most durable and chemical resistant?
   - ☐ A. Synthetic enamel.
   - ☐ B. Acrylic lacquer.
   - ☐ C. Polyurethane.

10. Aluminum-pigment in dope is used primarily to _____
    - ☐ A. provide a silver color.
    - ☐ B. aid in sealing out moisture from the fabric.
    - ☐ C. exclude sunlight from the fabric.

11. What could happen if the to be painted surface is not clean and free of any type of contaminants?
    - ☐ A. The surface has the appearance of orange peel.
    - ☐ B. The surface feels rough.
    - ☐ C. Fisheyes could appear on the surface.

AIRCRAFT PAINTING AND FINISHING

12. A rough surface that feels like sandpaper is an indication of _____
    - ☐ A. spray dust.
    - ☐ B. orange peel.
    - ☐ C. fisheyes.

13. What could happen if the paint material is not properly mixed?
    - ☐ A. Fisheyes.
    - ☐ B. Orange peel.
    - ☐ C. Wrinkles.

14. The registration marks must be at least _____ inches high. A glider may display marks at least _____ inches.
    - ☐ A. 8 inches, 4 inches.
    - ☐ B. 10 inches, 6 inches.
    - ☐ C. 12 inches, 3 inches.

15. The pressure used for a HVLP spray gun is _____ the pressure used for a traditional spray gun.
    - ☐ A. lower than
    - ☐ B. higher than
    - ☐ C. equal to

16. A spray gun that uses lower pressure and higher volumes of air is called _____
    - ☐ A. HVLP spray gun.
    - ☐ B. siphon feed gun.
    - ☐ C. gravity feed gun.

17. With 12" high registration marks, what is the minimum space required for the registration mark N1683C?
    Notes: 2/3 × height = character width   1/6 × height = width for 1
            1/4 × 2/3 height = spacing   1/6 × height = stroke or line width
    - ☐ A. 52 inches
    - ☐ B. 48 inches
    - ☐ C. 57 inches

18. A wash primer is a priming agent _____
    - ☐ A. that rinses off easily with water.
    - ☐ B. that has been thinned to a very light consistency.
    - ☐ C. that is only used as a second priming coat.

19. Orange peel can be caused by _____
    - ☐ A. overspray.
    - ☐ B. too much thinner added to the paint.
    - ☐ C. the thinner evaporating too quickly.

20. Polyurethane differs from lacquers and basic enamels in that _____
    - ☐ A. enamels and lacquers may not be thinned.
    - ☐ B. the first coat of polyurethane must be applied by a brush.
    - ☐ C. polyurethane requires a catalyst.

Chapter 8, Final Chapter Exam - Aircraft Painting and Finishing

Name:_____   Date:_____

AIRCRAFT ELECTRICAL SYSTEM

CHAPTER 9

Section A
Study Aid Questions - Fill In The Blanks

1. Ohm's Law describes the basic _____ relationships of _____.

2. Materials with a resistance to current flow halfway between the best conductor and the best insulators are called _____. Their application is in the field of _____.

3. Almost all mechanical devices, such as _____ and _____, use electromagnetic induction to produce electrical power.

4. According to Fleming's left hand rule the thumb represents _____, the index finger represents _____, and the middle finger denotes _____.

5. DC systems that require AC current use a(n) _____ to make the switch from 24V DC to 400 _____ current in order to operate specialty equipment.

6. _____ reactance and _____ reactance oppose current flow in AC circuits. They may also create a _____ shift between voltage and current.

7. Capacitance of parallel plates is _____ proportional to the distance between the plates. Therefore, if the distance doubles the capacitance is _____ by _____.

8. In an AC circuit where there is no inductance or capacitance, _____ is equal to the _____ of the circuit.

9. Two main types of batteries include _____ and _____. They are identified by the material used for the _____.

10. The emergency rate is the total _____ required to support the essential bus for _____ minutes.

11. Unlike lead-acid batteries, the state of charge of a Ni-Cad battery cannot be determined by measuring the specific gravity of the _____ electrolyte. State of charge is found by measuring the _____ with a Ni-Cad battery charger and following the _____.

12. In a series wound DC generator, when load increases, the voltage _____. This is because the greater the current through the field coils to the external circuit, the _____ the induced EMF and the _____ the output voltage.

13. DC generator control systems are often referred to as voltage regulators or _____. They are designed to keep the generator _____ within limits for all flight condition.

14. DC alternators contain two major components including the _____ winding and the _____ winding. Using the process of _____ induction, voltage is produced and fed to the aircraft electrical _____ and current is produced to power any electrical _____.

AIRCRAFT ELECTRICAL SYSTEM

15. A solid state regulator monitors DC alternator output _____ and controls alternator _____ current.

16. Inverters are _____ devices that convert DC power to _____. DC power feeds power to an AC distribution _____ that can be either 26 or 115 volts.

17. Constant speed drives can either be an independent unit or mounted within the _____. A dual CSD and alternator is known as a(n) _____.

18. AC alternator controls that measure the integrity of the electrical system include the _____ (BPCU) and the _____ (GCU).

19. A warning horn, with the gear switch in the up position, sounds when the _____ is reduced past a certain threshold and when the gear squat switch is _____.

20. Due to inflight vibration and _____, conductor wire should be _____ to minimize fatigue breakage.

21. Insulation resistance can be measured with a _____ or insulation tester, although it may not give a true picture of the _____ of the insulation.

22. The amount of current _____ is a function of the number of wires in the bundle and the _____ of the total wire bundle capacity that is being used.

23. Circuit resistance can be determined by checking the _____ across the circuit. As long as this value does not exceed the limit set down by the manufacturer, the resistance value for the circuit is considered _____.

24. There should be no more than _____ splice(s) in any one wire segment between two connectors. Splices in bundles must be _____ as to minimize any increase in bundle size.

25. _____ are devices that open and close circuits and they consist of one or more pair of contacts. Current is permitted to flow when these contacts _____.

AIRCRAFT ELECTRICAL SYSTEM

Matching

1. Match these diagram types with their descriptions below:

   A. Wiring Diagrams   B. Block Diagrams   C. Pictorial Diagrams   D. Schematic Diagrams

   _____ 1. Picture of the components used instead of conventional electrical symbols.

   _____ 2. Indicates the location of components with respect to each other.

   _____ 3. Consists of blocks that represent several components.

   _____ 4. Illustrates principle of operation.

   _____ 5. Identifies each component within a system by its part and serial number.

   _____ 6. Aid in troubleshooting complex electrical systems.

2. Match these switch types with their descriptions below:

   A. Switches   B. Electromagnetic Switches   C. Current Limiters

   _____ 1. Double-Pole Single-Throw   _____ 4. Fuse

   _____ 2. Relay   _____ 5. Toggle And Rocker

   _____ 3. Solenoid   _____ 6. Circuit Breaker

3. Match these switch types with the description or diagram below:

   A. SPST   B. DPST   C. SPDT   D. DPDT

   _____ 1. Switch is on in both positions.   _____ 7.

   _____ 2. Activates two separate circuits at the same time.   _____ 8.

   _____ 3. Switch routes current through either of the two paths.   _____ 9.

   _____ 4. Turns two circuits ON & OFF with one lever.

   _____ 5. Open and closes a single circuit.   _____ 10.

   _____ 6. May have a center "OFF" position.

AIRCRAFT ELECTRICAL SYSTEM

4. Match these aircraft lighting types with the descriptions below:

   A. Anti-Collision Lights C. Landing and Taxi Lights E. Inspection Lights
   B. Position Lights D. Wing

   _____ 1. Lights positioned in recessed areas of the wing designed to illuminate the ground.

   _____ 2. Rotating beam lights installed on the top of the fuselage or tail.

   _____ 3. Consists of one red, one green, and one white light.

   _____ 4. Lights that illuminate the leading edge of the wings.

   _____ 5. Has a white light located on the vertical stabilizer.

   _____ 6. Considered a safety light.

   _____ 7. Very powerful light directed by a parabolic reflector.

5. Match these functions with their descriptions below:

   A. Voltage Regulation D. Overexcitation Protection
   B. Overvoltage Protection E. Differential Voltage
   C. Parallel General Operations F. Reverse Current Sensing

   _____ 1. Ensures all generator voltage values are within a close tolerance before load is brought online.

   _____ 2. Adjusts the voltage regulation circuit to ensure all generators operate within limits.

   _____ 3. Adjusts field current to control generator output.

   _____ 4. Disconnects a generator from a bus in the event it becomes inoperative.

   _____ 5. Controls a generator that is out of limits due to a paralleled system failure.

   _____ 6. Opens the relay that controls the field excitation current.

6. Place the order of sequence of these events from start to finish (from A through F):

   _____ 1. Pilot exciter field creates a magnetic field and induces power in the pilot exciter field.

   _____ 2. Via EMF, main alternator field generates power in the main armature.

   _____ 3. Output of exciter armature is rectified.

   _____ 4. ACU receives power output from 1 of the armatures and sends it to the exciter field.

   _____ 5. Output of main AC armature is 3 phase AC.

   _____ 6. Exciter permanent magnet and armature start process.

Chapter 9, Section A - Aircraft Electrical System

Name:_____   Date:_____

AIRCRAFT ELECTRICAL SYSTEM

Section B
Knowledge Application Questions

1. A circuit with a 10Ω lamp and a 24V DC battery has a current of how many amps?

2. What is the resistance of a lamp in a circuit with a 12V DC battery and a current value of 3 amps?

3. What is the system voltage of a circuit with a resistance of 3.5Ω and a total current of 6.85A?

4. What is the effective value of the voltage if the peak value is 24V?

5. What is the peak value of the voltage if the effective voltage is 112V?

6. Referring to the diagram below; in an AC circuit with an inductance value of .175 Henrys and voltage of 110V at 60 cycles per second, what is the inductive reactance?

7. Referring to the diagram below, what is the impedance of the following circuit?

AIRCRAFT ELECTRICAL SYSTEM

8. Referring to the diagram below and the relationship between impedance, resistance, and reactance, find the total impedance of the following circuit.

9. Referring to the diagram below; find the total impedance of the following circuit.

10. What is the equation for True Power?

11. What is the unit for T.P.?

12. Referring to the diagram below, what is the total impedance of the following parallel AC circuit?

13. What is the equation for Apparent Power?

14. What is the unit for A.P.?

AIRCRAFT ELECTRICAL SYSTEM

15. Referring to the circuit diagram below, find TP, AP, and PF. (RT=5.6Ω)

16. Using the chart (Figure 9-2); determine the wire size for the following conditions:
    - Voltage Source 115V, Continuous Operation
    - Conduit
    - Wire Run of 160 ft.
    - 10A Load Capacity

WIRE SIZE
Voltage drop chart
Continuous flow at 20°
Tin-plated MIL-W-27759 conductor

NOTE
Length (LI) is based on conductor temperature of 20 °C.
To determine length (L2) at a higher conductor temperature, use formula in which T2 = estimated conductor temperature °C.

$$L2 = \frac{(254.5)(L1)}{(234.5)+(T2)}$$

Figure 9-2.

AIRCRAFT ELECTRICAL SYSTEM

17. Using the chart (Figure 9-2; Page 83); determine the wire size considering the following:
    - Voltage Source 14V, Continuous Operation
    - Conduit
    - Wire Run Length of 7Ft
    - 7A Load Capacity

18. Using chart (Figure 9-3); determine the wire size considering the following:
    - Voltage 28V, Intermittent Flow
    - Conduit
    - Wire Run of 24'
    - 10A Load

Figure 9-3.

AIRCRAFT ELECTRICAL SYSTEM

19. Using chart (Figure 9-4); What is the free air rating of a size 18 wire at an ambient temperature of 70°C and rated at 195°C?
    195-70 = 125; Wire Size #18

20. Using chart (Figure 9-4); What is the free air rating of a #22 wire at an ambient temperature of 40°C and rated at 200°C?
    200-40 = 160; Wire Size #22

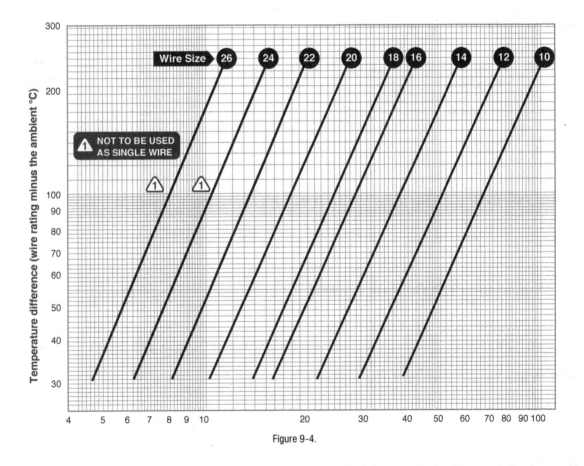

Figure 9-4.

21. What type of circuit breaker should not be used in aircraft?

AIRCRAFT ELECTRICAL SYSTEM

22. When should a switch be derated from its nominal rating?

23. What factors are considered when selecting wire size for electrical power?

24. When do DC motors draw several times their rated current?

25. How long should bonding jumper wires be?

26. When is a circuit breaker designed to open?

27. 27. How many terminal lugs can be put on a single stud on a terminal strip in an aircraft?

28. How can a particular wire in a bundle be identified?

29. What controls the output voltage of an alternator?

30. What size electrical conduit should be used?

Chapter 9, Section B - Aircraft Electrical System

Name:_____ Date:_____

AIRCRAFT ELECTRICAL SYSTEM

Section C
Final Chapter Exam

1. The effective value in an AC system has the same value as which of the following _____
   - ☐ A. the root mean square of the instantaneous voltage.
   - ☐ B. peak values of the sine wave.
   - ☐ C. 1.41 × peak voltage.

2. What are the terms used to describe wave lengths that are out of phase with one another?
   - ☐ A. Lead and lag.
   - ☐ B. Forward and aft.
   - ☐ C. Positive and negative.

3. What is inductance?
   - ☐ A. The total opposition to current flow.
   - ☐ B. A coils ability to hold an electric charge.
   - ☐ C. A coils ability to resist any change in current through it.

4. What is capacitive reactance?
   - ☐ A. The opposition to current flow due to the rate of charge of the circuit.
   - ☐ B. Rate of charge of the circuit.
   - ☐ C. The phase shift caused by the charging of a capacitor.

5. How can the overall battery condition be checked?
   - ☐ A. Load check.
   - ☐ B. Closed circuit voltage.
   - ☐ C. Resistance check.

6. Where is the voltage induced in a DC generator?
   - ☐ A. Armature
   - ☐ B. Slip rings
   - ☐ C. Stator

7. Why are the poles laminated?
   - ☐ A. Reduces arching.
   - ☐ B. Reduce eddy current loses.
   - ☐ C. Prolongs the life of poles.

8. How is the compound DC generator connected?
   - ☐ A. Field windings in series and in parallel.
   - ☐ B. Field winding in series, armature in parallel.
   - ☐ C. Armature in series, field winding in series.

9. What is the downside to series generators?
   - ☐ A. Poor voltage regulation.
   - ☐ B. They require a field rheostat.
   - ☐ C. The "coming in" speed is higher than that of parallel or compound.

10. How is the voltage in a shunt generator controlled?
    - ☐ A. Resistor
    - ☐ B. Capacitor
    - ☐ C. Rheostat

11. Modern GCUs for high output generators use what type of electronic circuits to sense operations?
    - ☐ A. Loop circuits.
    - ☐ B. Closed circuits.
    - ☐ C. Solid state circuits.

AIRCRAFT ELECTRICAL SYSTEM

12. What voltage sensitive device is found in almost all voltage regulating circuitry?
    - ☐ A. Zener diode.
    - ☐ B. Excitation relay.
    - ☐ C. Solenoid.

13. How many wire coils does a typical DC alternator have?
    - ☐ A. One
    - ☐ B. Two
    - ☐ C. Three

14. Why are ACU's considered more reliable than vibrating-type regulators?
    - ☐ A. No moving parts.
    - ☐ B. Do not require transistor circuitry to control current.
    - ☐ C. Provide addition protection like over and under current protection.

15. Which of the following is the proper symbol for a diode?
    - ☐ A. —▶|—
    - ☐ B. —⍉⍉⍉—
    - ☐ C. —▷—

16. The exciter generator in an AC alternator contains which of the following?
    - ☐ A. Armature and permanent magnet.
    - ☐ B. Armature and field winding.
    - ☐ C. Armature and field windings.

17. How does the speed control unit of a CSD adjust the hydraulic pressure to control output speed?
    - ☐ A. Piston pump
    - ☐ B. Wobble plate
    - ☐ C. Valve assembly

18. Why are starter motors controlled through a solenoid?
    - ☐ A. To prevent damage in case of starter malfunction.
    - ☐ B. To prevent a reverse polarity connection.
    - ☐ C. High amperage draw required for start.

19. (Refer to Figure 9-5; Page 94) When the "gear up" switches are in the not up position where does current flow through?
    - ☐ A. Though terminal 2, the squat switch, and the down solenoid.
    - ☐ B. Through terminal 1, the squat switch, and the up solenoid.
    - ☐ C. Through terminal 2, the squat switch, and the up solenoid.

20. (Refer to Figure 9-5; Page 94) What happens when the squat switch is activated (ground) and the gear switch is in the up position?
    - ☐ A. The gear will not retract.
    - ☐ B. The gear will not retract and a warning horn will sound.
    - ☐ C. The gear will retract.

21. (Refer to Figure 9-6; Page 95) What contacts must be closed for the APU gen to power AC bus 1?
    - ☐ A. APB, GB1
    - ☐ B. APB, BTB1
    - ☐ C. APB, BTB2

22. (Refer to Figure 9-6; Page 95) In the event that all generators fail, AC is available through which of the following _____
    - ☐ A. AC ESS INV.
    - ☐ B. AC ESS.
    - ☐ C. STAT INV.

AIRCRAFT ELECTRICAL SYSTEM

23. What dertermines the size of an aluminum conductor wire?
    - ☐ A. Current rating
    - ☐ B. Contact current rating
    - ☐ C. Termination hardware rating.

24. Which type of switch is spring loaded?
    - ☐ A. Toggle
    - ☐ B. Micro
    - ☐ C. Rocker

25. (Refer to Figure 9-7; Page 95) What generator powers the ESS AC BUS during normal operation?
    - ☐ A. Gen 1
    - ☐ B. Gen 2
    - ☐ C. Gen 3

Chapter 9, Final Chapter Exam - Aircraft Electrical System

Name:_____   Date:_____

AIRCRAFT ELECTRICAL SYSTEM

Figure 9-5.

AIRCRAFT ELECTRICAL SYSTEM

Figure 9-6.

Figure 9-7.

AIRCRAFT ELECTRICAL SYSTEM

PAGE LEFT BLANK INTENTIONALLY

AIRCRAFT INSTRUMENT SYSTEMS

CHAPTER 10

Section A
Study Aid Questions - Fill In The Blanks

1. There are usually two parts to any instrument or instrument system. One part _____ the situation and another part to _____ it.

2. Original analogue flight instruments are operated by _____ pressure and the use of _____ .

3. Three fundamental pressure-sensing mechanisms used in aircraft instrument are the _____ , the _____ , and the _____ sensing device.

4. Modern high performance aircraft use a digital air data computer that converts _____ into _____ .

5. ADCs receive input from the _____ sensing devices and process them for use by numerous _____ .

6. Altimeters that measure an aircraft's _____ by measuring _____ of the atmosphere are known as _____ altimeters.

7. Digital flight instruments perform all of the calculations for _____ in the ADC.

8. Many high performance aircraft are equipped with _____ for monitoring Mcrit.

9. A _____ is an electric system used for transmitting information from one point to another.

10. Autosyn systems are distinguished from Magnasyn systems by the fact that the transmitter and indicator rotors used are _____ magnets rather than _____ magnets.

AIRCRAFT INSTRUMENT SYSTEMS

11. The tachometer indicates the speed of the _____ of a reciprocating engine.

12. Some turbine engines use _____ for RPM indication, rather than _____ system.

13. An accelerometer is used to monitor _____ acting upon an airframe and are used in _____ navigation systems.

14. Modern aircraft AOA sensors units send output signals to the _____ .

15. Solid state magnetometers can not only sense the _____ to the earth magnetic poles, but also the _____ of the flux field.

16. Gyro instruments are driven by: _____ , _____ or _____ .

17. The attitude indicator, or _____ , provides _____ and _____ information.

18. Automatic pilot systems are capable of keeping aircraft stabilized _____ , _____ , and _____ .

19. The four basic components of an autopilot system are:

    1.

    2.

    3.

    4.

AIRCRAFT INSTRUMENT SYSTEMS

20. The Electronic Attitude Director Indicator (EADI) is an advanced version of _____ and _____ indicators.

21. The _____ system automatically monitors the airframe and engine systems and alerts the flight crew in case of a system failure.

22. The highest level of automated flight system is the _____.

23. The FMS coordinates the adjustment of _____, _____, and _____ parameters either automatically or by instructing the pilot how to do so.

24. When an aircraft is to be operational under IFR, an altimeter test must have been performed within the previous _____ months.

25. Compass magnetic deviation is caused by _____ interference from ferrous materials and operating _____ components in the cockpit.

Section A
True of False

_____ 1. Direct sensing instruments sense and display the information all in one instrument.

_____ 2. The three basic kinds of instruments are classified as: flight instruments, engine instruments, and environmental control instruments.

_____ 3. In a Bourdon tube the higher the pressure of the fluid, the more the tube straightens.

_____ 4. Many flight instruments use a Bourdon type of sensing device.

_____ 5. Solid state pressure sensing systems are internal sensing systems.

_____ 6. The Engine Pressure Indicator (EPR) compares the total exhaust pressure to the pressure of the ram air at the inlet of the engine.

_____ 7. True airspeed is the relationship between the ram air pressure and static air pressure.

_____ 8. The calculations of calibrated airspeed for modern aircraft with digital instruments are performed by the Air Data Computer (ADC).

_____ 9. Aircraft with Direct Current (DC) systems often use synchro systems for transmitting information from one point to another.

_____ 10. Tachometers used for turbine engines monitor the speed of the compressor section of the engine.

AIRCRAFT INSTRUMENT SYSTEMS

True of False (continued)

_____ 11. Two types of Angle of Attack sensors used in aircraft are the vane type which uses an alpha vane externally mounted to the outside of the fuselage and the other type uses two slots in a probe that extends out of the side of the fuselage.

_____ 12. Some AOA systems incorporate a stick pusher actuator that pushes the control yoke backwards to lower the nose of the aircraft.

_____ 13. Two common application of thermocouples are: cylinder head temperature in reciprocating engines and exhaust gas temperature in turbine engines.

_____ 14. Total air temperature (TAT) is the static air temperature minus any lowering in temperature caused by flying at high altitudes.

_____ 15. Magnetic deviation, variation, and dip errors are errors associated with a magnetic compass?

_____ 16. The process for knowing how to adjust for magnetic variation is known as swinging the compass.

_____ 17. Ring Laser Gyros (RLG), Microelectromechanical systems, and Attitude Heading and Reference Systems (AHRS) are examples of attitude and directional systems used on modern aircraft.

_____ 18. The sensing elements of an autopilot system are: the attitude and directional gyros, the turn coordinator, magnetic compass, and an altitude control.

_____ 19. The output elements of an autopilot system are the servos that cause actuation of the flight control surfaces.

_____ 20. The electronic flight instrument system replaces the attitude indicator and vertical gyro by cathode ray tubes (CRT) or LCDs that display EADI and EHSI presentations.

_____ 21. The EICAS monitors engine and airframe parameters and doesn't utilize traditional gauges.

_____ 22. Maintenance personnel can access the EICAS to access data related to a failure event.

_____ 23. The master caution lights on the enunciator panel can not be canceled by the flight crew.

_____ 24. Instrument panels are usually shock mounted to absorb high frequency, high-amplitude shocks.

_____ 25. The original equipment manufacturer will put colored range markings on the instrument face in accordance with the type certificate data sheet.

Chapter 10, Section A - Aircraft Instrument Systems

Name:_____ Date:_____

AIRCRAFT INSTRUMENT SYSTEMS

Section B
Knowledge Application Questions

1. What is used as a reference for range marking instruments?

2. What does a yellow arc on an instrument dial indicate?

3. What aircraft instrument may be used to check a manifold pressure indicator for correct indication?

4. What indication errors may be found in altimeters?

5. What flight instruments are usually connected to a pitot-static system?

6. What is required after replacement of components connected to a pitot-static system?

7. What methods are used to drive turn-and-bank indicators?

AIRCRAFT INSTRUMENT SYSTEMS

8. What is a synchro-type remote indicating system?

9. What does a tachometer indicate?

10. What type of indicating system is used to measure the turbine-engine exhaust gas temperature?

11. What is the meaning of swinging a compass?

12. Name the three types of basic instruments used in an aircraft flight station?

    1.

    2.

    3.

13. What does an Engine Pressure Indicator (EPR) compare?

14. What equipment performs the calculation of calibrated airspeed for modern aircraft with digital instruments?

AIRCRAFT INSTRUMENT SYSTEMS

15. Describe the two types of Angle of Attack sensors used in aircraft.

    1.

    2.

16. What are the two most common applications of thermocouples?

    1.

    2.

17. What type of system does monitor engine and airframe parameters and does not utilize traditional gauges.

18. What system can be accessed by maintenance personnel to access data related to a failure event.

19. What type of instrument maintenance can be performed by certificated A&P mechanics?

20. Name at three systems or components that provide input to the Flight Management Computer (FMC)?

    1.

    2.

    3.

Chapter 10, Section B - Aircraft Instrument Systems

Name:_____ Date:_____

AIRCRAFT INSTRUMENT SYSTEMS

PAGE LEFT BLANK INTENTIONALLY

AIRCRAFT INSTRUMENT SYSTEMS

Section C
Final Chapter Exam

1. Aircraft instrument panels are generally shock mounted to absorb _____
   - ☐ A. all vibration.
   - ☐ B. low frequency, high amplitude shocks.
   - ☐ C. high frequency, high amplitude shocks.

2. Aircraft instruments should be marked and graduated in accordance with _____
   - ☐ A. the instrument manufacturer's specifications.
   - ☐ B. both the aircraft and engine manufacturers' specifications.
   - ☐ C. the specific aircraft maintenance or flight manual.

3. What marking color is used to indicate if a cover glass has slipped?
   - ☐ A. Red
   - ☐ B. White
   - ☐ C. Yellow

4. The green arc on an aircraft temperature gauge indicates _____
   - ☐ A. the instrument is not calibrated.
   - ☐ B. the desirable temperature range.
   - ☐ C. a low, unsafe temperature range.

5. An aircraft instrument panel is electrically bonded to the aircraft structure to _____
   - ☐ A. act as a restraint strap.
   - ☐ B. provide current return paths.
   - ☐ C. aid in the panel installation.

6. A radar altimeter indicates _____
   - ☐ A. flight level (pressure) altitude.
   - ☐ B. altitude above sea level.
   - ☐ C. altitude above ground level.

7. When installing an instrument in an aircraft, who is responsible for making sure it is properly marked?
   - ☐ A. The aircraft owner.
   - ☐ B. The instrument installer.
   - ☐ C. The instrument manufacturer.

8. A certificated mechanic with airframe and powerplant ratings may _____
   - ☐ A. perform minor repairs to aircraft instruments.
   - ☐ B. perform minor repairs and minor alterations to aircraft instruments.
   - ☐ C. not perform repairs to aircraft instruments.

9. Which instrument is connected only to an aircraft's static pressure system?
   - ☐ A. Altimeter.
   - ☐ B. Airspeed indicator.
   - ☐ C. Cabin altimeter.

10. If a static pressure system check reveals excessive leakage, the leak(s) may be located by _____
    - ☐ A. pressurizing the system and adding leak detection dye.
    - ☐ B. isolating portions of the line and testing each portion systematically, starting at the instrument connections.
    - ☐ C. removing and visually inspecting the line segments.

11. The red radial lines on the face of an engine oil pressure gauge indicates _____
    - ☐ A. minimum engine safe RPM operating range.
    - ☐ B. minimum precautionary safe operating range.
    - ☐ C. minimum and/or maximum safe operating limits.

AIRCRAFT INSTRUMENT SYSTEMS

12. An aircraft magnetic compass is swung to update the compass correction card when _____
    - ☐ A. an annual inspection is accomplished on the aircraft.
    - ☐ B. the compass is serviced.
    - ☐ C. equipment is added that could effect compass deviation.

13. When swinging a magnetic compass, the compensator's are adjusted to correct for _____
    - ☐ A. magnetic influence deviation.
    - ☐ B. compass card oscillations.
    - ☐ C. magnetic variations.

14. The maximum altitude loss permitted during an unpressurized aircraft instrument static pressure system integrity check is _____
    - ☐ A. 50 feet in 1 minute.
    - ☐ B. 200 feet in 1 minute.
    - ☐ C. 100 feet in 1 minute.

15. A barometric altimeter indicates pressure altitude when the barometric scale is set at _____
    - ☐ A. 29.92 inches Hg.
    - ☐ B. 14.7 inches Hg.
    - ☐ C. Field elevation.

16. The function of a CRT in an EFIS is to _____
    - ☐ A. allow the pilot to select the appropriate system configuration for the current flight situation.
    - ☐ B. display alphanumeric data and representations of aircraft instruments.
    - ☐ C. receive and process input signals from the aircraft and engine sensors, and send the data to the appropriate display.

17. Who is authorized to repair an aircraft instrument?
    01. A certified mechanic with an airframe rating.
    02. A certificated repairman with an airframe rating.
    03. A certificated repair station approved for that class instrument.
    04. A certificated airframe repair station.
    - ☐ A. 01, 02, 03, and 04
    - ☐ B. 03 and 04
    - ☐ C. 03

18. A synchro transmitter is connected to a synchro receiver _____
    - ☐ A. mechanically through linkage.
    - ☐ B. electromagnetically without wires.
    - ☐ C. electrically with wires.

19. A turn coordinator instrument indicates _____
    - ☐ A. the longitudinal attitude of the aircraft during climb and descent.
    - ☐ B. both roll and yaw.
    - ☐ C. the need for corrections in pitch and bank.

20. What does a reciprocating engine manifold pressure gauge indicate when the engine is not operating?
    - ☐ A. Zero pressure.
    - ☐ B. The differential between the manifold pressure and the atmospheric pressure.
    - ☐ C. The existing atmospheric pressure.

21. The Flight Management System coordinates the adjustment of _____
    - ☐ A. flight parameters only.
    - ☐ B. engine parameters only.
    - ☐ C. engine parameters, flight parameters, airframe parameters.

22. The system that automatically monitors the airframe and engine systems and alerts the flight crew in case of a system failure is called _____
    - ☐ A. EADI.
    - ☐ B. AFCS.
    - ☐ C. ECAM.

23. An accelerometer is used to monitor _____ acting upon an airframe.
    - ☐ A. pressures
    - ☐ B. forces
    - ☐ C. airflow

24. The Engine Pressure Indicator (EPR) compares _____
    - ☐ A. the total exhaust pressure to the pressure of the ram air at the inlet of the engine.
    - ☐ B. the total manifold pressure to the pressure at the inlet of the engine.
    - ☐ C. the total turbine pressure to the pressure of the ram air at the inlet of the engine

25. What system can be accessed by maintenance personnel to access data related to a failure event?
    - ☐ A. ADC
    - ☐ B. EICAS
    - ☐ C. EFIS

Chapter 10, Final Chapter Exam - Aircraft Instrument Systems

Name:_____   Date:_____

AIRCRAFT INSTRUMENT SYSTEMS

PAGE LEFT BLANK INTENTIONALLY

COMMUNICATION AND NAVIGATION

CHAPTER 11

Section A
Study Aid Questions - Fill In The Blanks

1. Covalent bonds are created when two or more substances share electrons in their _____.

2. Electron flow occurs when there are _____ in the valence shell due to the atom's preference to have _____ electrons in all of its shell.

3. A four-layer diode or _____ has three junctions. The behavior of the junctions can be understood by considering it to be two interconnected _____ transistors.

4. SCRs are often used in high _____ situations, such as switching, phase controls, battery chargers, and _____ circuits.

5. The _____ and amount of voltage applied to the gate can widen and narrow the _____ due to expansion or shrinkage of the depletion area at the junction of the semiconductor.

6. Depletion mode MOSFETs are considered normally _____ while enhanced mode MOSFETZs are normally _____.

7. Forward biased _____ give off energy visible in the _____ characteristic unique to the material of the semiconductor being used.

8. Transistors are rated by the _____ of the collector current to the _____ current, or Beta.

9. Common-_____ amplifiers are unique because their construction creates a situation where the base current is _____ than the collector or emitter current.

10. If there is to be an output voltage in a _____ gate, then the inputs cannot both have voltage.

11. The primary flight display displays the attitude indicator in the _____ half of the display and the electronic _____ indicator on the other half.

12. The electronic field component and the electromagnetic field component are oriented _____ to each other and at _____ to the direction that the wave is traveling.

COMMUNICATION AND NAVIGATION

13. Two common methods of modulating _____ waves are amplitude and _____ modulation.

14. FM is considered _____ to AM for carrying and deciphering information on _____ waves.

15. The information signal is separated from the carrier wave portion of the signal by the _____.

16. Antennas are _____. They radiate and receive waves in certain patterns and _____.

17. _____ wire is used to connect transmitters and receivers to their _____.

18. VORs are marked on aeronautical charts along with their name, the _____ to tune, and a _____ designator.

19. On an RDF system, the only way to determine if the aircraft was flying to or from the _____ was the increasing and decreasing strength of the _____ signal.

20. The combination of a magnetic compass, VOR, and ADF into one instrument is found on an _____.

21. Vertical guidance required for an aircraft to descend for landing is provided by the _____ at an angle of about _____.

22. A _____ transponder provides positive identification and _____ of an aircraft on the radar screen of ATC.

23. Traffic collision _____ systems, or TCAS, are _____ based air-to-air traffic monitoring and alerting systems.

24. The _____ covering the antenna must only be painted with approved paint to allow radio signals to pass unobstructed.

25. The GPS receiver measures the time it takes for a signal to arrive from _____ transmitting satellites. This two dimensional position is expressed in _____ coordinates.

COMMUNICATION AND NAVIGATION

Section A
True of False

_____ 1. Maintenance of avionics is typically done by a technician with an Airframe license.

_____ 2. Analog representations are discontinuous.

_____ 3. Diodes act as check valves in AC circuits.

_____ 4. Tetrodes are used at higher frequencies than triodes.

_____ 5. Semiconductors are thought to be the building blocks of modern electronics.

_____ 6. A material is an insulator if the electrons in the valence shell are allowed to move freely from one shell to another.

_____ 7. N-type semiconductor material is also known as a donor material.

_____ 8. The amount of current that is allowed to pass through a forward biased diode is indirectly proportional to the amount of voltage applied.

_____ 9. A transistor is a sandwich of N-type material between two pieces of P-type material and vice versa.

_____ 10. Current to the collector-emitter is turned on and off by the voltage applied to the collector.

_____ 11. Photodiodes can carry more current than a photon activated transistor.

_____ 12. Rectifiers change AC voltage to DC voltage.

_____ 13. Common-emitter circuits are characterized by high power gains.

_____ 14. A sine wave is produced by generators when an conductor is rotated in a uniform electric field.

_____ 15. Digital logic is based on the binary numbering system.

_____ 16. All gates are amplifiers subject to output fluctuations.

_____ 17. The negative OR gate is the same as the NOR gate.

_____ 18. The relationship between frequency and wavelength is directly proportional.

_____ 19. Ground waves are useful for long distance transmissions.

_____ 20. VHF communication radios range from 118.0MHz to 336.975MHz.

_____ 21. The distance a carrier wave travels is directly related to the amplification of the signal sent to the antenna.

_____ 22. Most radio transmitters generate an unstable oscillating frequency that is stabilized by a mixer.

_____ 23. A transceiver is a communication radio that transmits and receives.

_____ 24. The strongest signals received align directly with the length of the antenna.

_____ 25. The course deviation indicator on an OBS is essentially vertical but moves right and left across graduations each representing 5° of course deviation.

_____ 26. The VOR circuitry is still active on an VOR/ILS receiver when the ILS localizer frequency is tuned in.

8083-31B-ATB Airframe Workbook

COMMUNICATION AND NAVIGATION

True of False (continued)

_____ 27. DME distances are slant distances which is longer than ground distance.

_____ 28. Transponder code 7700 is used for hijack situations.

_____ 29. A radio altimeter indicates altitude in MSL.

_____ 30. The accuracy of GPS is within 20 meters horizontally and can be improved to 7.6 meters with the integration of WAAS to the GPS.

Chapter 11, Section A - Communication and Navigation

Name:_____   Date:_____

COMMUNICATION AND NAVIGATION

Section B
Knowledge Application Questions

1. How are analog electric signals modified?

2. Why were vacuum tubes replaced by solid-state devices in aircraft radios?

3. Why is silicon one of the primary materials used in the manufacturing of semi-conductors?

4. When is a semi-conductor said to be reversed biased and what is the resulting effect of the circuit?

5. What does it mean when a diode is designed with a zener voltage and why are they used?

6. What are the advantages of a UJT over a bipolar transistor?

7. What are Shockley diodes useful for?

8. What are the three basic amplifier types?

    1.

    2.

    3.

COMMUNICATION AND NAVIGATION

9. Explain what a NOT gate does in terms of Logic in and out and what this means in relation to voltage.

10. What is the difference between an EXCLUSIVE OR and an OR?

11. Explain the processes of transmitting radio waves.

12. What is demodulation in amplitude modulation?

13. Why is frequency modulation considered superior to amplitude modulation?

14. What are the 3 frequencies produced when two AC signals are mixed together?

    1.

    2.

    3.

15. What is the purpose of the receiver and what does it do?

16. What are the three characteristics of concern when considering an antenna?

17. How is the use of one-quarter of the wavelength antenna possible?

COMMUNICATION AND NAVIGATION

18. What is antenna field directivity?

19. Describe the difference between dipole, Marconi, and loop antennas.

20. How does a VOR receiver interpret the signal generated by the VOR station?

21. Describe each of the radio transmissions used on an ILS approach.

22. What does pressing IDENT do for an ATC controller?

23. When is TCAS II required and what does it provide?

24. What are the advantages of ADS-B over conventional ground-based radar?

25. What are the 3 segments of GPS?

   1.

   2.

   3.

Chapter 11, Section B - Communication and Navigation

Name:_____ Date:_____

COMMUNICATION AND NAVIGATION

26. What is the most common communication system in use?

27. How often does the ATC transponder require certification?

28. Why are two antennas or a single multi-element antenna usually required for an ILS system?

29. What information does a glide slope radio beam provide?

30. What is one method used to monitor the output signal during an ELT test?

COMMUNICATION AND NAVIGATION

Section C
Final Chapter Exam

1. As of 1994, how many satellites currently make up the global positioning system?
   - ☐ A. 15
   - ☐ B. 24
   - ☐ C. 35

2. Which of the follow is an advantage of digital electronics over analog electronics?
   - ☐ A. Continuously voltage modification.
   - ☐ B. Easily modified by small inputs.
   - ☐ C. Better noise control.

3. What happens to electrons when they are heated?
   - ☐ A. Expand their orbit.
   - ☐ B. Contract their orbit.
   - ☐ C. Nothing.

4. What does a triode contain that a diode does not?
   - ☐ A. Heater
   - ☐ B. Grid
   - ☐ C. Screen Grid

5. How is the screen grid powered?
   - ☐ A. Positive DC voltage.
   - ☐ B. Positive AC voltage.
   - ☐ C. Negative AC voltage.

6. A negatively doped semi-conductor is bonded to what type of element?
   - ☐ A. An element with 5 valence electrons.
   - ☐ B. An element with 3 valence electrons.
   - ☐ C. An element with 4 valence electrons.

7. The ease with which electron movement occurs at a given voltage is affected by which of the following _____
   - ☐ A. heat.
   - ☐ B. polarity.
   - ☐ C. conductivity of material.

8. Current does not flow through a transistor unless _____
   - ☐ A. voltage is applied to the base, narrowing the depletion area at the base-emitter.
   - ☐ B. voltage is applied to the collector, narrowing the depletion area at the collector-base.
   - ☐ C. voltage is applied to the emitter, widening the depletion area at the base-emitter.

9. Which of the following is a characteristic of an SCR?
   - ☐ A. Has a Zener voltage.
   - ☐ B. Has a break over voltage rather than a breakdown voltage.
   - ☐ C. Limit current flow to one direction.

10. A uni-junction transistor does not have which of the following _____
    - ☐ A. base material.
    - ☐ B. collector material.
    - ☐ C. emitter material.

11. A three-phase AC circuit is rectified with a _____
    - ☐ A. 3 diode circuit.
    - ☐ B. 4 diode circuit.
    - ☐ C. 6 diode circuit.

COMMUNICATION AND NAVIGATION

12. Common-collector circuits are characterized by _____
    - ☐ A. high current gain and 180° voltage phase shift from input to output.
    - ☐ B. high current gain but practically no voltage gain.
    - ☐ C. attenuates current but causes a high gain in voltage.

13. A tank circuit is one with _____
    - ☐ A. a capacitor and coil in parallel with one another.
    - ☐ B. a capacitor and coil in series with one another.
    - ☐ C. a capacitor and resistor in parallel with one another.

14. The output of a negative AND gate is the same as a(n) _____
    - ☐ A. EXCLUSIVE OR.
    - ☐ B. NAND.
    - ☐ C. NOR.

15. What are the frequency ranges and names given to VLF, LF, and MF waves?
    - ☐ A. 3kHZ-3mHZ, ground waves.
    - ☐ B. 2MHz-25MHz, surface waves.
    - ☐ C. 3kHz-30mHz, sky waves.

16. Which of the following frequencies contain the information signal after it comes out of the mixer?
    - ☐ A. Radio frequency.
    - ☐ B. Local oscillator frequency.
    - ☐ C. Difference frequency.

17. How can radio antennas be made effectively shorter?
    - ☐ A. Adding a properly rated capacitor in series with the transmission line.
    - ☐ B. Adding an inducer in the circuit.
    - ☐ C. Both A and B.

18. For optimum performance, the impedance of the transmission line should be equal to the impedance of the antenna, which is often _____
    - ☐ A. 5 ohms.
    - ☐ B. 50 ohms.
    - ☐ C. 75 ohms.

19. When is the reference signal of a VOR in phase with the variable signal?
    - ☐ A. Magnetic North
    - ☐ B. 90°
    - ☐ C. 180°

20. Where are VOR receivers operationally tested and what is the maximum acceptable error?
    - ☐ A. VOT, ±2°
    - ☐ B. Avionics Repair Station, ±4°
    - ☐ C. VOT, ±4°

21. Which of the following lights represents a marker beacon signal?
    - ☐ A. Blue
    - ☐ B. Amber
    - ☐ C. White

22. According to Title 14 CFR 91 section 91.413, all transponders on aircraft flown in controlled airspace are required to be inspected and tested every _____
    - ☐ A. 30 days.
    - ☐ B. 12 calendar months.
    - ☐ C. 24 calendar months.

COMMUNICATION AND NAVIGATION

23. Magenta is reserved for which of the following onboard weather radar receivers?
    - ☐ A. Heavy precipitation.
    - ☐ B. Extreme precipitation.
    - ☐ C. Wind shear.

24. Which of the following provides an actual return on weather radar?
    - ☐ A. Severe turbulence.
    - ☐ B. Wind shear.
    - ☐ C. Hail.

25. How are separation minimums reduced for precision approaches?
    - ☐ A. GPS equipped aircraft.
    - ☐ B. WAAS equipped aircraft.
    - ☐ C. IRS equipped aircraft.

Chapter 11, Final Chapter Exam - Communication and Navigation

Name:_____ Date:_____

COMMUNICATION AND NAVIGATION

PAGE LEFT BLANK INTENTIONALLY

HYDRAULIC AND PNEUMATIC POWER SYSTEMS

CHAPTER 12

Section A
Study Aid Questions - Fill In The Blanks

1. Hydraulic operations are roughly _____ % efficient, with _____ loss due to fluid friction.

2. The 3 principle categories of hydraulic fluids are: _____, _____, and _____ base.

3. Phosphate ester based fluids are used mostly in transport category aircraft which is commonly referred to as _____. Presently, type _____ and _____ are used exclusively.

4. Hydraulic systems require special accessories such as _____, _____, and _____ to be compatible with the fluid being used.

5. Filter ratings are given in terms of _____, and is an indication of the _____ size that will be filtered out.

6. Differential pressure indicators are designed to prevent false indications due to _____, _____, or _____.

7. Power packs are driven by either a(n) _____ or _____.

8. Reservoirs can be pressurized or _____. Commercial transport aircraft have pressurized reservoirs and most of them use _____ to do this.

9. A filter is a(n) _____ or _____ device used to clean the hydraulic fluid, thus _____ foreign contaminates from remaining in the system.

10. Maintenance of filters is relatively easy. It consists mostly of _____ the filter and element or cleaning the filter and _____ the element.

11. _____ pressure provides a convenient means of monitoring the condition of installed filter elements. It is the _____ used in the differential pressure or _____ filter indicators found on many filter assemblies.

12. Once extended, the differential pressure indicator must be _____ and provides a _____ warning of a loaded element.

13. All aircraft hydraulic systems have one or more _____ pumps and may have a(n) _____ pump as an additional unit when the _____ pump is inoperative.

14. Pumps may be classified in 1 of 2 categories: _____ or _____ displacement.

HYDRAULIC AND PNEUMATIC POWER SYSTEMS

15. The _____ section of the drive coupling, located _____ of the two sets of splines, is _____ in diameter than the splines.

16. Most valves are _____ controlled by a(n) _____ and are sometimes called _____ valves.

17. A sequence valve _____ fluid to a second actuator or motor after a set _____ has been reached, to do work in another part of the system.

18. A(n) _____ will give precedence to the critical hydraulic sub systems over _____ systems when system pressure is _____.

19. Fuses detect sudden increase in flow such as a(n) _____ downstream, which in turn, _____ hydraulic fluid for the rest of the system.

20. Pressure relief valves are necessary to prevent _____ of components or _____ of hydraulic lines under _____ pressure.

21. _____ relief valves are used to relieve excessive pressure that may exist due to _____ of the fluid.

22. Pressure _____ are devices used to manage the output of the _____ to maintain system operating pressure within a fixed range.

23. The main purpose of the _____ valve is to isolate the normal system from an alternate or emergency system. The sliding component of this valve is to _____ either one of the other inlet ports.

24. Shut off valves are used to shut off the flow of fluid to a particular _____ or _____.

25. The initial charge of an operational accumulator is known as _____.

122 8083-31B-ATB Airframe Workbook

HYDRAULIC AND PNEUMATIC POWER SYSTEMS

Section A
True of False

_____ 1. Large transport category aircraft hydraulic systems produce around 500 psi of pressure.

_____ 2. Both a high flash point and a high fire point are desirable for hydraulic fluids.

_____ 3. The only contaminants that really affect a hydraulic system are abrasive type contaminants (ex. sand, rust, and machining chips)

_____ 4. If the system becomes contaminated, it must to be purged immediately.

_____ 5. Basic hydraulic systems have one of the following: directional valve, check valve, pressure relief valve, or selector valve.

_____ 6. A hydraulic power pack does not require a centralized hydraulic power supply or long hydraulic lines.

_____ 7. Pressurized reservoirs use quantity transmitters to gauge fluid quantity in the system.

_____ 8. The micron element is designed to prevent passage of solids greater than 1 micron in size.

_____ 9. Thermal lockout devices incorporated into some button indicators prevent operation of the indicator below a certain temperature.

_____ 10. Most modern power-driven pumps are variable-delivery, compressor-controlled type.

_____ 11. All aircraft axial-piston pumps have an odd number of pistons (5, 7, 9, etc.).

_____ 12. When the pump outlet pressure of a Vickers variable delivery pump is below 2,850 psi, it is held at its maximum angle in relation with the drive shaft centerline by the force of the yoke return spring.

_____ 13. There are two types of inline check valves: simple-type and orifice-type.

_____ 14. Automatic resetting fuses are designed to allow a certain volume of fluid per minute to pass through.

_____ 15. An accumulator is a steel sphere divided into two chambers by a rubber diaphragm.

Chapter 12, Section A - Hydraulic and Pneumatic Power Systems

Name:_____ Date:_____

HYDRAULIC AND PNEUMATIC POWER SYSTEMS

PAGE LEFT BLANK INTENTIONALLY

HYDRAULIC AND PNEUMATIC POWER SYSTEMS

Section B
Knowledge Application Questions

1. What are three types of hydraulic fluids?

2. What could happen when Skydrol® spills onto plastic resins, vinyl compositions, lacquers and oil base paints?

3. What feature is built into the drive shaft of a hydraulic pump to prevent engine damage in the event of pump seizure or overload?

4. What maintenance action is required to minimize contamination during replacement of a hydraulic unit?

5. What condition will cause the filter by-pass on a hydraulic filter to open and allow in unfiltered fluid?

6. Name four types of hydraulic pumps?

    1.

    2.

    3.

    4.

7. What sources could pressurize a pressurized hydraulic reservoir?

8. What is the purpose of a pressure relief valve?

HYDRAULIC AND PNEUMATIC POWER SYSTEMS

9. What is the purpose of a pressure regulator?

10. What is used in some hydraulic systems to supplement the power pump output during high demand?

11. What is the purpose of restrictors that are used in aircraft pneumatic systems?

12. Why should a pneumatic system be purged periodically?

13. What must be accomplished with an accumulator prior to disassembling?

14. Can different hydraulic fluid types be mixed? Why?

15. Why do most aircraft hydraulic installations require a closed center hydraulic system?

16. What is the advantage of a powerpack hydraulic system?

17. Why are hydraulic reservoirs of many transport type aircraft pressurized?

18. Explain the principle of operation of a filter by-pass valve.

HYDRAULIC AND PNEUMATIC POWER SYSTEMS

19. Name two examples of non-positive displacement pumps.

    1.

    2.

20. (Refer to Figure 12-1; below). What happens when the control pressure (Pc) increases?

21. (Refer to Figure 12-1; below) What happens when the pressure adjustment screw will be turned clockwise?

22. How are sequence valves controlled?

Figure 12-1.

HYDRAULIC AND PNEUMATIC POWER SYSTEMS

23. What is the function of the power transfer unit used in large aircraft hydraulic systems?

24. (Refer to Figure 12-2; below) What will happen if the EDV solenoid will be energized?

25. What is the reason for using pressure reducing valves?

Figure 12-2.

HYDRAULIC AND PNEUMATIC POWER SYSTEMS

26. What are the functions of an accumulator?

27. What is the function of the Ram Air Turbine that is often installed in large transport type aircraft?

28. What is pneudraulics?

29. (Refer to Figure 12-3; below) What will happen if the fluid level in the reservoir drops below the standpipe?

Figure 12-3.

Chapter 12, Section B - Hydraulic and Pneumatic Power Systems

Name:_____ Date:_____

8083-31B-ATB Airframe Workbook

HYDRAULIC AND PNEUMATIC POWER SYSTEMS

PAGE LEFT BLANK INTENTIONALLY

HYDRAULIC AND PNEUMATIC POWER SYSTEMS

Section C
Study Aid Questions - Final Chapter Exam

1. What are the main subsystems of every hydraulic system?
   - ☐ A. Pump, reservoir, accumulator, heat exchanger, and filtering system.
   - ☐ B. Pump, transfer pump, reservoir, heat exchanger, and filtering system.
   - ☐ C. Pump, carburetor, accumulator, heat exchanger, and filtering system.

2. Which property should be considered when choosing a fluid for a given hydraulic system?
   - ☐ A. Color.
   - ☐ B. Flash point.
   - ☐ C. Dew point.

3. Which of the following seals is compatible with Skydrol®?
   - ☐ A. Buna N.
   - ☐ B. Neoprene.
   - ☐ C. Butyl rubbe

4. During maintenance and servicing procedures, all parts should be washed in _____
   - ☐ A. solvent.
   - ☐ B. MEK.
   - ☐ C. soap and water.

5. Where are filters installed in the hydraulic system?
   - ☐ A. Pressure lines, Return lines, pump case drain lines.
   - ☐ B. Pressure lines, Return lines, reservoir drain lines.
   - ☐ C. Return lines, pump case drain lines, reservoir drain lines.

6. What type of hydraulic pump is used with an open center hydraulic system?
   - ☐ A. Constant displacement pump.
   - ☐ B. Variable displacement pump.
   - ☐ C. Centrifugal pump.

7. If a constant delivery pump is used in a closed system, how is system pressure regulated?
   - ☐ A. Pump's integral pressure mechanism.
   - ☐ B. Pressure regulator.
   - ☐ C. Relief valve.

8. What is the advantage of an open system over a closed system?
   - ☐ A. Continuous pressurization.
   - ☐ B. Faster operation of the system.
   - ☐ C. Gradual pressure buildup.

9. What is a function of a hydraulic reservoir?
   - ☐ A. Purges air bubbles.
   - ☐ B. Heats the hydraulic fluid.
   - ☐ C. Filters the hydraulic fluid.

10. How and why are non-pressurized reservoirs kept under a slight pressure?
    - ☐ A. Thermal expansion, eliminates foaming and air in the system.
    - ☐ B. Bleed air, ensures positive fluid flow.
    - ☐ C. Thermal expansion, ensures positive fluid flow.

11. How are high altitude aircraft hydraulic system reservoirs pressurized?
    - ☐ A. Purges air bubbles.
    - ☐ B. Heats the hydraulic fluid.
    - ☐ C. Filters the hydraulic fluid.

8083-31B-ATB Airframe Workbook

HYDRAULIC AND PNEUMATIC POWER SYSTEMS

12. How can contamination be minimized while adding fluid to the reservoir?
    - ☐ A. Close manual vent valve.
    - ☐ B. Use of a hydraulic filler unit.
    - ☐ C. Pour clean fluid directly into the reservoir.

13. Inline filter assemblies are comprised of what three basic units?
    - ☐ A. Head assembly, bowl, element.
    - ☐ B. Head assembly, module, element.
    - ☐ C. Connecting lines, module, micron filter.

14. Which type of filter is designed to be thrown away after removal from the system?
    - ☐ A. Magnetic type.
    - ☐ B. Porous metal.
    - ☐ C. Micron.

15. Power driven pumps can be categorized as _____
    - ☐ A. Engine driven, air driven, electric driven.
    - ☐ B. Engine driven, air driven, mechanical actuated.
    - ☐ C. Air driven, electric driven, mechanical actuated.

16. What type of pump has two mesh gears that revolve in a housing driven by an engine or power unit?
    - ☐ A. Gear pump.
    - ☐ B. Gerotor pump.
    - ☐ C. Piston pump.

17. What type of pump has two crescent shaped openings?
    - ☐ A. Gerotor pump.
    - ☐ B. Piston pump.
    - ☐ C. Vane pump.

18. How is displacement determined by piston pumps?
    - ☐ A. Diameter of the pistons and the stroke length.
    - ☐ B. Diameter of the pistons, stroke length, and number of pistons.
    - ☐ C. Stroke length and number of pistons.

19. How is the pump output changed to accommodate pressure demands in a variable-delivery pump?
    - ☐ A. Pump compensator.
    - ☐ B. Internal pressure changes.
    - ☐ C. Centrifugal type vanes.

20. What is the purpose of a selector valve?
    - ☐ A. Allows flow in one direction with no or restricted flow in the opposite direction.
    - ☐ B. Switches fluid flow through an actuator.
    - ☐ C. Enables one unit to automatically set another unit into motion.

21. What is the purpose of a check valve?
    - ☐ A. Allows flow in one direction with no or restricted flow in the opposite direction.
    - ☐ B. Converts mechanical motion into one requiring greater power.
    - ☐ C. Switches fluid flow through an actuator.

22. Which check valve allows for restricted flow in the opposite direction when closed, and how it is accomplished?
    - ☐ A. Simple-type using a ball and spring.
    - ☐ B. Orifice-type using a ball and spring.
    - ☐ C. Orifice-type using a damping valve.

23. Why are safety relief valves used in hydraulic systems?
    - ☐ A. To limit the maximum system pressure to protect the system.
    - ☐ B. To regulate system pressure.
    - ☐ C. To drain the hydraulic system during maintenance.

HYDRAULIC AND PNEUMATIC POWER SYSTEMS

24. What is used when a hydraulic system's pressure must be lowered to a specific amount?
    - ☐ A. Pressure reducing valve.
    - ☐ B. Pressure relief valve.
    - ☐ C. Pressure regulating valve.

25. What is the purpose of a sequence valve?
    - ☐ A. Allows flow in one direction with no or restricted flow in the opposite direction.
    - ☐ B. Converts mechanical motion into one requiring greater power.
    - ☐ C. Enables one unit to automatically set another unit into motion.

Chapter 12, Final Chapter Exam - Hydraulic and Pneumatic Power Systems

Name:_____ Date:_____

HYDRAULIC AND PNEUMATIC POWER SYSTEMS

PAGE LEFT BLANK INTENTIONALLY

AIRCRAFT LANDING GEAR SYSTEMS

CHAPTER 13

Section A
Study Aid Questions - Fill In The Blanks

1. Name the three basic arrangements of landing gear used in aircraft.

    1.   2.   3.

2. Parasite drag caused by landing gear can be reduced by the addition of _____, or _____.

3. Most single engine aircraft use a non-shock absorbing landing gear made from _____, _____, or _____.

4. To keep the shock strut and wheels aligned, most shock struts are equipped with _____, and _____.

5. Nose gear shock struts have a _____ to keep the gear aligned when the aircraft takes off and the shock strut fully extend.

6. The alignment of a main wheel in the vertical plain is called _____.

7. The electric/hydraulic landing gear system found in many Cessna and Piper aircraft is called a _____.

8. The _____ lowers the landing gear if the main power system fails.

9. The proper functioning of a landing gear system and components can be checked by performing a _____. This is also known as _____ gear.

10. Nose wheel vibration is controlled through the use of a _____.

AIRCRAFT LANDING GEAR SYSTEMS

11. The inner wheel halve of a wheel used on a high performance aircraft is likely to have one or more _____.

12. All aircraft axle nuts must be installed and _____ in accordance with the airframe manufacturer's maintenance procedures.

13. Overheating of the wheel bearings could be caused by a _____ and results in a _____ tint to the metal surface.

14. Brinelling is caused by _____. It appears as _____ in the bearing cup raceway.

15. Pushing the _____ of the right rudder pedal activates the brake on the _____ main wheel.

16. The _____ transfers the motions of the pistons to the stack of _____ and _____ to slow the rotation of the wheel.

17. The _____ is the latest iteration of the multiple disc brake.

18. The three brake actuating systems used are _____, _____ and _____.

19. Power brake systems use the _____ as the source of power to apply the brakes.

20. The auto brake system is used to stop the wheels automatically after _____ this prevents the wheels from rotating when retracted in the wheel wells.

21. The anti-skid system not only detects wheel _____, it also detects when wheel skid is _____.

AIRCRAFT LANDING GEAR SYSTEMS

22. Maximum braking efficiency exists when the wheels are decelerating at a maximum rate but are not _____ .

23. Brake systems with master cylinders may be bled by _____ or _____ bleeding methods.

24. A flat spot on a tire is the result of the tire _____ on the runway surface.

25. Operation on a grooved runway can cause an aircraft tire tread to develop shallow _____ shaped cuts.

Section A
True of False

_____ 1. Most aircraft with a tricycle landing gear use differential braking for steering during ground operations.

_____ 2. When more than two wheels are attached to a landing gear strut, the attaching mechanism is known as a bogie.

_____ 3. Landing gear shock struts are filled with air and synthetic turbine engine oil.

_____ 4. During taxi operations the air in the tires and the hydraulic fluid in the shock strut combine to smooth out bumps.

_____ 5. To check the fluid level of most shock struts, the strut needs to be deflated and fully compressed.

_____ 6. Most smaller aircraft use a powerpack gear retraction system while large aircraft use a hydraulic landing gear retraction system.

_____ 7. Sequence valves are often operated mechanically and priority valves control gear component timing via hydraulic volume adjustments.

_____ 8. Some aircraft use a mechanical emergency release system that unlocks the uplocks and the gear will free fall, while others use a pneumatic power system to lower the gear when the main system fails.

_____ 9. Proximity sensors are used for gear position safety switches on many smaller single engine aircraft.

_____ 10. The most common display for the landing gear being up and locked is an illuminated green light.

_____ 11. Aircraft equipped with a hydraulic nose wheel steering system utilize the steering cylinders as shimmy dampers.

_____ 12. Wheels for modern aircraft use a one piece design which provides superior strength and ease of tire installation.

_____ 13. The two pieces of a two piece aircraft wheel are identical and could be used on both the inside as outside of the wheel assembly.

AIRCRAFT LANDING GEAR SYSTEMS

True of False (continued)

_____ 14. Aircraft technicians should be careful when they approach or remove a tire. The high internal pressure of the tire can create a catastrophic failure that could be lethal to the technician.

_____ 15. In a fixed disk brake system (Cleveland) the brake caliper and linings adjust their position in relationship to the disc.

_____ 16. Dual disc brakes are used on large transport category aircraft that use hydraulic systems to operate the brake systems.

_____ 17. In general small light aircraft use independent brake systems. A master cylinder provides the hydraulic pressure.

_____ 18. The brake accumulator is an emergency source of power for the brake system.

_____ 19. Autobrake systems on large aircraft do not use the anti-skid system to control wheel skid.

_____ 20. In order to bleed the power brake system of a large transport category aircraft the hydraulic system needs to be pressurized.

_____ 21. Type III tires are common general aviation tires, Type V tires are high performance tires found on jet aircraft.

_____ 22. Traditional aircraft tires are bias ply tires while modern large aircraft utilize radial tires.

_____ 23. When checking tire pressure wait at least 30 minutes after a typical landing to ensure the tire has cooled to ambient temperature.

_____ 24. Small pieces of rock or debris can be removed with a probing tool or screwdriver while the tire is on the aircraft and inflated.

_____ 25. Under inflation could be evident from excessive wear on the outside of the tire threads.

Chapter 13, Section A - Aircraft Landing Gear Systems

Name:_____   Date:_____

AIRCRAFT LANDING GEAR SYSTEMS

Section B
Knowledge Application Questions

1. What is used to service an air/oil landing gear shock strut?

2. What regular inspection should be made of the exposed portion of a landing gear strut?

3. What is the purpose of main landing gear torque links and arms?

4. What power sources are normally used to retract landing gear systems?

5. What type of nosewheel steering is provided on small aircraft?

6. What unit prevents nosewheel vibrations?

7. What is the purpose of power brake debooster cylinders?

8. Name the common types of brake systems used on aircraft?

9. What must be accomplished before inspecting a wheel brake system for hydraulic leaks?

AIRCRAFT LANDING GEAR SYSTEMS

10. What prevents a split wheel from leaking air through the inner and outer mating surfaces, or the wheel assembly?

11. What is the most important maintenance action for safe, long, aircraft tire service?

12. What are the effects of under inflation on tires?

13. When should a landing gear retraction check be accomplished?

14. What is the indication of excessive heating of a wheel bearing?

15. What is the purpose of an anti-skid system?

16. What is the purpose of a wheel fusible plug?

17. What are some methods of bleeding brakes?

18. What methods are used for transmitting the brake pedal movements to a steering control unit in large aircraft?

19. What prevents a nose landing gear from being retracted with the nosewheel out of the center position?

AIRCRAFT LANDING GEAR SYSTEMS

20. What type of material is used for modern brake rotors on transport category aircraft?

21. What are two different configurations of landing gear?

22. Describe a spring steel landing gear.

23. What is the difference between spring-oleo struts and air-oleo shock struts?

24. What is the purpose of the metering pin in an air-oleo shock strut?

25. What features must a nose gear strut assembly have that are not required for main gear?

26. Describe a landing-gear truck assembly.

27. What are the four methods that may be used for the emergency extension of the landing gear?

28. With what type of landing gear are most helicopters equipped?

29. What markings are required on aircraft tires?

AIRCRAFT LANDING GEAR SYSTEMS

30. What is the advantage of having wheels constructed in two parts?

AIRCRAFT LANDING GEAR SYSTEMS

Section C
Final Chapter Exam

1. What should be checked when a shock strut bottoms during a landing?
   - ☐ A. Air pressure.
   - ☐ B. Packing seals for correct installation.
   - ☐ C. Fluid level.

2. Overinflated aircraft tires may cause damage to the _____
   - ☐ A. brake linings.
   - ☐ B. wheel hub.
   - ☐ C. wheel flange.

3. What is the function of a cam incorporated in a nose gear shock strut?
   - ☐ A. Provides an internal shimmy damper.
   - ☐ B. Straightens the nosewheel.
   - ☐ C. Provides steering of aircraft during ground operation.

4. Debooster cylinders are used in brake systems primarily to _____
   - ☐ A. reduce brake pressure and maintain static pressure.
   - ☐ B. relieve excessive fluid and ensure a positive release.
   - ☐ C. reduce the pressure to the brake and increase the volume of fluid flow.

5. The purpose of a relief valve in a brake system is to _____
   - ☐ A. reduce pressure for brake application.
   - ☐ B. prevent the tire from skidding.
   - ☐ C. compensate for thermal expansion.

6. A high speed aircraft tire with a sound cord body and bead may be recapped _____
   - ☐ A. a maximum of three times.
   - ☐ B. only by the tire manufacturer.
   - ☐ C. an indefinite number of times.

7. The fusible plugs installed in some aircraft wheels will _____
   - ☐ A. indicate tire tread separation.
   - ☐ B. prevent over inflation.
   - ☐ C. melt at a specified elevated temperature.

8. Instructions concerning the type of fluid and amount of air pressure to be put in a shock strut are found _____
   - ☐ A. on the airplane data plate.
   - ☐ B. in the aircraft operations limitations.
   - ☐ C. in the aircraft manufacturer's service manual.

9. The primary purpose for balancing aircraft wheel assemblies is to _____
   - ☐ A. prevent heavy spots and reduce vibration.
   - ☐ B. distribute the aircraft weight properly.
   - ☐ C. reduce excessive wear and turbulence.

10. The pressure source for power brakes is _____
    - ☐ A. the main hydraulic system.
    - ☐ B. the power brake reservoir.
    - ☐ C. a master cylinder.

11. What is the purpose of the torque links attached to the cylinder and piston of a landing gear oleo strut?
    - ☐ A. Limit compression stroke.
    - ☐ B. Hold the strut in place.
    - ☐ C. Maintain correct wheel alignment.

AIRCRAFT LANDING GEAR SYSTEMS

12. When an air/oil type of landing gear shock strut is used, the initial shock of landing is cushioned by _____
    - ☐ A. compression of the air charge.
    - ☐ B. the fluid being forced through a metered opening.
    - ☐ C. compression of the fluid.

13. The purpose of a sequence valve in a hydraulic retractable landing gear system is to _____
    - ☐ A. prevent heavy landing gear from falling too rapidly upon extension.
    - ☐ B. provide a means of disconnecting the normal source of hydraulic power and connecting the emergency source of power.
    - ☐ C. ensure operation of the landing gear and gear doors in the proper order.

14. Nose gear centering cams are used in many retractable landing gear systems. The primary purpose of the centering device is to _____
    - ☐ A. align the nosewheel prior to touchdown.
    - ☐ B. engage the nosewheel steering.
    - ☐ C. center the nosewheel before it enters the wheel well.

15. How long should you wait after a flight before checking tire pressure?
    - ☐ A. At least 3 hours.
    - ☐ B. At least 2 hours.
    - ☐ C. At least 30 minutes.

16. An electric motor used to raise and lower a landing gear would most likely be a _____
    - ☐ A. shunt field series wound motor.
    - ☐ B. split field shunt wound motor.
    - ☐ C. split field series wound motor.

17. A landing gear position and warning system will provide a warning in the cockpit when the throttle is _____
    - ☐ A. retarded and gear is not down and locked.
    - ☐ B. advanced and gear is down and locked.
    - ☐ C. retarded and gear is down and locked.

18. Excessive wear in the center of the tread of an aircraft tire is an indication of _____
    - ☐ A. incorrect camber.
    - ☐ B. excessive toe out.
    - ☐ C. over inflation.

19. On most aircraft, the oil level of an air and oil shock strut is checked by _____
    - ☐ A. removing the oil filler plug and inserting a gauge.
    - ☐ B. measuring the length of the strut extension with a certain air pressure in the strut.
    - ☐ C. releasing the air and seeing that the oil is to the level of the filler plug.

20. How can it be determined that all air has been purged from a master cylinder brake system?
    - ☐ A. By operating a hydraulic unit and watching the system pressure gauge for smooth, full scale deflection.
    - ☐ B. By noting whether the brake is firm or spongy.
    - ☐ C. By noting the amount of fluid return to the master cylinder upon brake release.

21. Aircraft brakes requiring a large volume of fluid to operate the brakes generally _____
    - ☐ A. use independent master cylinder systems.
    - ☐ B. do not use brake system accumulators.
    - ☐ C. use power brake control valves.

22. To prevent a very rapid extension of an oleo shock strut after initial compression resulting from landing impact _____
    - ☐ A. various types of valves or orifices are used which restrict the reverse fluid flow.
    - ☐ B. the metering pin gradually reduces the size of the orifice as the shock strut extends.
    - ☐ C. the air is forced through a restricted orifice in the reverse direction.

AIRCRAFT LANDING GEAR SYSTEMS

23. The metering pins in oleo shock struts serve to _____
    - ☐ A. lock the struts in the DOWN position.
    - ☐ B. retard the flow of oil as the struts are compressed.
    - ☐ C. meter the proper amount of air in the struts.

24. After performing maintenance on an aircraft's landing gear system which may have affected the system's operation, it is usually necessary to _____
    - ☐ A. conduct a flight test.
    - ☐ B. re-inspect the area after the first flight.
    - ☐ C. make an operational check with the aircraft on jacks.

25. Why do tire and wheel manufacturers often recommend that the tires on split rim wheels be deflated before removing the wheel from the axle?
    - ☐ A. To relieve the strain on the wheel retaining nut and axle threads.
    - ☐ B. As a safety precaution in case the bolts that hold the wheel halves together have been damaged or weakened.
    - ☐ C. To remove the static load imposed upon the wheel bearings by the inflated tire.

Chapter 13, Final Chapter Exam - Aircraft Landing Gear Systems

Name:_____ Date:_____

8083-31B-ATB Airframe Workbook

AIRCRAFT LANDING GEAR SYSTEMS

PAGE LEFT BLANK INTENTIONALLY

AIRCRAFT FUEL SYSTEM

CHAPTER 14

Section A
Study Aid Questions - Fill In The Blanks

1. Fuel with low volatility could cause _____, _____, and _____ acceleration.

2. Gasoline must truly burn rather than _____ or _____.

3. Vapor lock is a condition in which AVGAS _____ in a fuel line or other component between the fuel tank and the _____.

4. Carburetor icing is most common at ambient temperatures of _____ but can occur at much higher temperatures especially in _____ conditions.

5. Detonation is the rapid, uncontrolled _____ of fuel due to high _____, and _____.

6. Turbine engine fuels have _____ volatility and _____ boiling points than gasoline.

7. Large transport category aircraft use often three types of fuel tanks. They are:

   _____   _____   _____

8. There are three types of aircraft fuel tanks. They are:

   _____   _____   _____

9. Aircraft fuel tanks have a low area called a _____ that is designed as a place for contaminants and water to settle.

10. Always route a fuel line below any _____.

11. The most common electric motor operated fuel valves are the _____ valve and the _____ type valve.

12. A characteristic of solenoid operated fuel valves is that they open and close _____.

13. The boost pump delivers fuel under positive pressure to the _____.

14. Centrifugal fuel boost pumps used in aircraft with reciprocating engines ensure _____ pressure and are preventing _____.

15. Reciprocating engine aircraft typically use a _____ engine driven fuel pump.

8083-31B-ATB Airframe Workbook

AIRCRAFT FUEL SYSTEM

16. Fuel boost pumps on many large aircraft are used for several different fuel sub systems such as a _____ , and _____ system.

17. Fuel strainers are designed to trap _____ pieces of debris and prevent their passage through the _____ .

18. _____ filters are commonly used on turbine powered aircraft. This type of filter captures extremely fine particles in the range of _____ microns.

19. _____ are used in turbine powered aircraft to prevent the formation of ice in the fuel.

20. Modern aircraft use electric fuel quantity indicators which operate with _____ current.

21. Four basic classifications are used to describe aircraft fuel leaks. They are:

    _____   _____   _____   _____

22. Heavy seeps are classified as an area of fuel from _____ to _____ in diameter that forms in 30 minutes.

23. When an integral fuel cell needs to be repaired the tank needs to _____ and tested with a _____ to be certain it can be entered safely.

24. Unstrained water can be detected by a _____ appearance to the fuel.

25. Two types of fueling processes are: _____ and _____ .

Section A
True of False

_____ 1. A fuel jettison system is required on aircraft that have a higher take off weight than landing weight.

_____ 2. Turbine fuel has a much lower flash point than AVGAS.

_____ 3. Vapor lock can be caused by excessively hot fuel, low pressure, or excessive turbulence of the fuel traveling through the fuel system.

_____ 4. Detonation could be recognized by a pinging or knocking sound and it causes a lower cylinder head temperature.

_____ 5. AVGAS 100LL could be distinguished from other fuels by its blue color.

_____ 6. Jet B fuel is the most common jet fuel in the United States and it allows engine restarts at high altitude.

_____ 7. Low and mid wing single reciprocating engine aircraft use a gravity fuel system.

_____ 8. Large transport type aircraft typically use integral fuel tanks in each of their wing structures to store the fuel.

_____ 9. A fuel transfer system allows fuel to be transferred from one fuel tank to another and a fuel cross feed system allows any engine to draw fuel from any tank.

AIRCRAFT FUEL SYSTEM

True of False (continued)

_____ 10. Aircraft equipped with integral fuel tanks do not have fuel vent systems instead they use fuel jettison systems to vent the fuel tanks.

_____ 11. Motor and solenoid operated valves used in a fuel system use position enunciator lights to indicate valve position in addition to the switch position.

_____ 12. The fuel boost pump delivers fuel under positive pressure to the fuel control.

_____ 13. A centrifugal boost pump is a constant displacement pump.

_____ 14. A sump is typically located in the highest part of the tank so that the water and contaminants can be drained before the flight.

_____ 15. The most common type of fuel heaters for large transport category aircraft are air/fuel heaters and oil/fuel heaters.

_____ 16. The flight crew uses information of the filter by-pass indicating lights and fuel temperature gauge to know when to turn the fuel heaters on or fuel heaters can work automatically

_____ 17. The disadvantage of electronic fuel quantity systems is that they have many moving components.

_____ 18. Many aircraft with capacitance type fuel indicating systems also use a mechanical indication system to cross check fuel quantity indications.

_____ 19. Fuel flow meters in turbine aircraft measure the volume of the fuel consumed by the engine.

_____ 20. A higher fuel flow indication should result in a higher exhaust gas temperature.

_____ 21. When fuel leaks into a confined area the leak must be monitored every flight.

_____ 22. Microorganisms appear as a visible slime that is dark brown, grey, red, or black in color.

_____ 23. The best solution to stop microorganisms to grow in AVGAS is to keep water from accumulating in the fuel.

_____ 24. The type of fuel to be used is placarded near the fill port on over-the-wing systems and at the fueling station on pressure refueled aircraft.

_____ 25. Aircraft fuel boost pumps can be used on some aircraft to defuel the tanks or the pump of the fuel truck can be used to defuel the airplane.

Chapter 14, Section A - Aircraft Fuel System

Name:_____   Date:_____

AIRCRAFT FUEL SYSTEM

PAGE LEFT BLANK INTENTIONALLY

AIRCRAFT FUEL SYSTEM

Section B
Knowledge Application Questions

1. What is the purpose of a fuel dump system incorporated in many transport category aircraft?

2. Name three types of fuel cells.

    1.   2.   3.

3. What supports the weight of fuel in a bladder-type fuel cell?

4. What is the purpose of a fuel temperature indicator in a turbine powered aircraft?

5. What is the purpose of a fuel crossfeed system in multiengine aircraft?

6. What three positions may be selected on a fuel tank selector valve?

    1.   2.   3.

7. What are drip gauges and sight gauges used for?

8. What type of fueling system is used on large transport category aircraft?

9. What are some advantages of single point pressure fueling?

AIRCRAFT FUEL SYSTEM

10. What method may be used to check a fuel tank for leaks after a patch or weld has been performed?

11. What type of fuel system leak will not be visible by evidence of stains or wet spots?

12. Name four types of fuel quantity gauges that are common?

    1.

    2.

    3.

    4.

13. Why is an electronic-type fuel quantity gauge more accurate than others?

14. What is the purpose of fuel tank internal baffles?

15. Why should you wait a period of time after fueling before checking fuel sumps?

16. What is the best way to stop microorganisms to grow in jet fuel?

17. Describe an integral fuel-tank design also called wet wing.

AIRCRAFT FUEL SYSTEM

18. How is a bladder fuel cell attached to the airframe?

19. What markings are required at the fuel filler cap location?

20. How does an ejector fuel pump work?

21. Describe a vane-type fuel pump.

22. Where are centrifugal fuel-boost pumps for aircraft usually located?

23. What indicators could be used to determine when there may be danger of ice crystals forming in

24. Explain the operation of a filter bypass warning system.

25. Why are fuel heaters necessary?

26. What are the purposes of a fuel vent system?

27. When would a fuel jettison system be required for small aircraft?

AIRCRAFT FUEL SYSTEM

28. What is an electrical operated fuel tank shutoff valve in-transit light?

29. Explain the purpose of a cross-feed system.

30. What should be done with old gaskets and seals when replacing fuel system components?

Chapter 14, Section B - Aircraft Fuel System

Name:_____   Date:_____

AIRCRAFT FUEL SYSTEM

Section C
Final Chapter Exam

1. Why are integral fuel tanks used in many large aircraft?
   - ☐ A. To reduce fire hazards.
   - ☐ B. To facilitate servicing.
   - ☐ C. To reduce weight.

2. Regarding the below statements, which is true?
   01. A fuel pressure relief valve is required on an aircraft positive displacement fuel pump.
   02. A fuel pressure relief valve is required on an aircraft centrifugal fuel boost pump.
   - ☐ A. Only No. 01 is true.
   - ☐ B. Only No. 02 is true.
   - ☐ C. Both No. 01 and No. 02 are true.

3. Aircraft defueling should be accomplished _____
   - ☐ A. with the aircraft's communication equipment on and in contact with the tower in case of fire.
   - ☐ B. in a hangar where activities can be controlled.
   - ☐ C. in the open air for good ventilation.

4. What method is used on turbine powered aircraft to determine when the condition of the fuel is approaching the danger of forming ice crystals?
   - ☐ A. Fuel pressure warning.
   - ☐ B. Fuel pressure gauge.
   - ☐ C. Fuel temperature indicator.

5. In an electronic type fuel quantity indicating system, the tank sensing unit is a _____
   - ☐ A. capacitor.
   - ☐ B. variable resistor.
   - ☐ C. variable inductor.

6. To prevent vapor lock in fuel lines at high altitude, some aircraft are equipped with _____
   - ☐ A. vapor separators.
   - ☐ B. direct injection type carburetors.
   - ☐ C. booster pumps.

7. If a bladder type fuel tank is to be left empty for an extended period of time, the inside of the tank should be coated with a film of _____
   - ☐ A. engine oil.
   - ☐ B. linseed oil.
   - ☐ C. ethylene glycol.

8. A fuel temperature indicator is located in the fuel tanks on some turbine powered airplanes to tell when the fuel may be _____
   - ☐ A. getting cold enough to form hard ice.
   - ☐ B. in danger of forming ice crystals.
   - ☐ C. about to form rime ice.

9. What type of fuel booster pump requires a pressure relief valve?
   - ☐ A. Concentric.
   - ☐ B. Vane.
   - ☐ C. Centrifugal.

10. According to Part 23, what minimum required markings must be placed at or near each appropriate fuel filler cover for reciprocating engine-powered airplanes?
    - ☐ A. The word 'Avgas' and the minimum fuel grade.
    - ☐ B. The word 'Fuel' and usable fuel capacity.
    - ☐ C. The word 'Avgas' and the total fuel capacity.

AIRCRAFT FUEL SYSTEM

11. Why is it necessary to vent all aircraft fuel tanks?
    - ☐ A. To ensure a positive head pressure for a submerged boost pump.
    - ☐ B. To exhaust fuel vapors.
    - ☐ C. To limit pressure differential between the tank and atmosphere.

12. Flapper valves are used in fuel tanks to _____
    - ☐ A. reduce pressure.
    - ☐ B. prevent a negative pressure.
    - ☐ C. act as check valves.

13. The use of turbine fuels in aircraft has resulted in some problems not normally associated with aviation gasoline. One of these problems is _____
    - ☐ A. increasing viscosity of fuel as fuel temperature lowers at altitude.
    - ☐ B. higher vapor pressure.
    - ☐ C. microbial contaminants.

14. What is the recommended practice for cleaning a fuel tank before welding?
    - ☐ A. Purge the tank with air.
    - ☐ B. Flush the inside of the tank with clean water.
    - ☐ C. Steam clean the tank interior.

15. Pressure fueling of aircraft is usually accomplished through _____
    - ☐ A. pressure connections on individual fuel tanks.
    - ☐ B. at least one single point connection.
    - ☐ C. individual fuel tank overwing and/or fuselage access points.

16. Aircraft pressure fueling systems instructional procedures are normally placarded on the _____
    - ☐ A. fuel control panel access door.
    - ☐ B. lower wing surface adjacent to the access door.
    - ☐ C. aircraft ground connection point.

17. What is the primary purpose of the cross feed system?
    - ☐ A. To allow the feeding of any engine from any tank.
    - ☐ B. To allow the feeding of fuel from one tank for defueling.
    - ☐ C. To provide automatic refueling of a tank to any desired level.

18. Fuel is moved overboard in most fuel jettison systems by _____
    - ☐ A. boost pumps.
    - ☐ B. gravity.
    - ☐ C. gravity and engine driven fuel pumps.

19. The primary purpose of an aircraft's fuel jettison system is to quickly achieve a _____
    - ☐ A. lower landing weight.
    - ☐ B. balanced fuel load.
    - ☐ C. reduced fire hazard.

20. Before fueling an aircraft with the pressure fueling method, what important precaution should be observed?
    - ☐ A. The truck pump pressure must be correct for that refueling system.
    - ☐ B. The truck pump pressure must be adjusted for minimum filter pressure.
    - ☐ C. The aircraft's electrical system must be on to indicate quantity gauge readings.

21. A capacitance type fuel quantity indicating system measures fuel in _____
    - ☐ A. pounds.
    - ☐ B. pounds per hour.
    - ☐ C. gallons.

22. Why is the capacitance fluid quantity system more accurate in measuring fuel level than a mechanical type?
    - ☐ A. Only one probe and one indicator are necessary for multiple tank configurations.
    - ☐ B. It measures in gallons and converts to pounds.
    - ☐ C. It measures by weight instead of volume.

23. A drip gauge may be used to measure _____
    - ☐ A. the amount of fuel in the tank.
    - ☐ B. system leakage with the system shut down.
    - ☐ C. fuel pump diaphragm leakage.

24. Why are jet fuels more susceptible to water contamination than aviation gasoline?
    - ☐ A. Jet fuel has a higher viscosity than gasoline.
    - ☐ B. Jet fuel is lighter than gasoline; therefore, water is more easily suspended.
    - ☐ C. Condensation is greater because of the higher volatility of jet fuels.

25. What method would check for internal leakage of a fuel valve without removing the valve from the aircraft?
    - ☐ A. Place the valve in the OFF position, drain the strainer bowl, and with boost pump on, watch to see if fuel flows to the strainer bowl.
    - ☐ B. Remove fuel cap(s), turn boost pump(s) on, and watch for bubbling in the tanks.
    - ☐ C. Apply air pressure on the downstream side of the fuel pump and listen for air passing through the valve.

Chapter 14, Final Chapter Exam - Aircraft Fuel System

Name: _____ Date: _____

AIRCRAFT FUEL SYSTEM

PAGE LEFT BLANK INTENTIONALLY

ICE AND RAIN PROTECTION

CHAPTER 15

Section A
Study Aid Questions - Fill In The Blanks

1. Under certain atmospheric conditions, ice can build rapidly on _____ and _____.

2. On days when there is visible _____ in the air, ice can form on aircraft leading edge surfaces at altitudes where _____ start.

3. Rime ice is _____ in weight than clear ice, and its weight is _____ significance.

4. _____ ice is brittle and more easily removed than _____ ice.

5. Whenever _____ conditions are encountered, the _____ characteristics of the airplane will _____.

6. The most common systems used to prevent icing on wing leading edges are _____, _____, and _____.

7. There are several methods used to provide heated air. These include bleeding hot air from the _____, _____, and ram air heated by a _____.

8. Modern aircraft use several onboard _____ to control anti-ice and deice aircraft systems.

9. _____ anti-icing systems are also often utilized for vertical and horizontal stabilizer anti-ice systems.

10. Chemical anti-icing systems are often called liquid freeze point depressant systems or _____ systems.

11. General Aviation (GA) aircraft and turboprop commuter type aircraft often use a _____ to break of the ice after it has formed on the _____ surfaces.

12. Wing deice boots are held against the airfoil surfaces by _____ from the _____ side of the pumps.

ICE AND RAIN PROTECTION

13. Deicer tubes are inflated by an _____, or by air bled from _____.

14. Propellers are deiced with _____ or _____ systems.

15. The electrical window heat system prevents _____ and _____ on the flight deck windows.

16. The windshields are heated by _____ embedded in the glass or by a _____ that is applied on the inside of the outer windshield ply.

17. Ice can be visibly detected but most modern aircraft have one or more _____ that warn the flight crew of icing conditions.

Section A
True of False

_____ 1. Clear ice forms a smooth sheet of solid ice.

_____ 2. Rime ice has a white appearance.

_____ 3. Ice buildup causes destructive vibration, and hampers true instrument readings.

_____ 4. Control surfaces become unbalanced or frozen due to the buildup of ice.

_____ 5. Radio reception is hampered and engine performance is affected due to the buildup of ice.

_____ 6. For the most part, general aviation aircraft equipped to fly in icing conditions use thermal or electric anti-icing systems that are controlled automatically to prevent the formation of ice.

_____ 7. Large transport category aircraft are equipped with advanced deicing boots.

_____ 8. Some modern large aircraft are using electrical thermal anti-icing systems.

_____ 9. A chemical anti-icing is strictly a anti-icing system to prevent the formation of ice and cannot be utilized as a deicing system.

_____ 10. Air pressure for a pneumatic wings deice system is supplied by the vacuum pump.

_____ 11. Engine driven air pumps are available in a wet and a dry-type and used with turbine engines.

_____ 12. Most general aviation aircraft are equipped with a dry-type of pump.

_____ 13. The deice control valve is normally energized and releases air from the vacuum pump overboard.

_____ 14. Frost deposits can be removed by placing the aircraft in a warm hangar or by using a deicing fluid.

_____ 15. The rain repellent system should not be operated on dry windows because heavy undiluted repellent will restrict window visibility.

Chapter 15, Section A - Ice and Rain Protection

Name: _____ Date: _____

ICE AND RAIN PROTECTION

ICE AND RAIN PROTECTION

PAGE LEFT BLANK INTENTIONALLY

ICE AND RAIN PROTECTION

Section B
Knowledge Application Questions

1. What are the two types of ice that are encountered during flight?

   1.   2.

2. What are the two basic hazards associated with ice or frost forming on aircraft?

   1.   2.

3. What could be the result of ice breaking of the wing and entering the engine intake?

4. Name the areas on an aircraft that could be equipped with deicing or anti-icing systems?

5. Name four types of systems that are used to prevent or control ice formation in aircraft?

   1.   3.

   2.   4.

6. Describe for what type of applications thermal anti-icing systems are used?

7. Why are the left and right wing anti-ice valves operated at the same time?

8. Explain why and how an electric thermal deicing system is made inoperative when the aircraft is on the ground?

9. Explain how a chemical anti-icing system works.

ICE AND RAIN PROTECTION

10. Explain how the pneumatic deice system in Figure 15-1 below works.

Figure 15-1.

11. Explain why the boot of a pneumatic deicing system should not stay inflated longer than 7 to 10 seconds?

12. Why do aircraft equipped with turbine engines use bleed air from the engine compressor?

13. What is the reason dry vacuum pumps do not need any lubricants?

14. What type of rain control systems are used on aircraft?

ICE AND RAIN PROTECTION

15. What are two methods of inflating pneumatic deicer boots?

16. What is the function of the oil separator used in some deicer boot systems?

17. Why is a conductive coating required for deicer boots?

18. What normally keeps deicer boots held down in flight?

19. What is the usual source of heat for thermal anti-icing?

20. How is the temperature maintained in a thermal anti-icing system?

21. What happens to the thermal anti-icing airflow after it has heated a leading edge surface?

22. Name at least two methods used to remove rain from a windshield?

23. What two power sources operate windshield wiper systems?

24. What are the two inherent problems associated with windshield wipers, when operated in flight?

ICE AND RAIN PROTECTION

25. How does a pneumatic rain removal system work?

Chapter 15, Section B - Ice and Rain Protection

Name:_____ Date:_____

ICE AND RAIN PROTECTION

Section C
Final Chapter Exam

1. Arcing in an electrically heated windshield panel usually indicates a breakdown in the _____
   - ☐ A. temperature sensing elements.
   - ☐ B. autotransformers.
   - ☐ C. conductive coating.

2. How do deicer boots help remove ice accumulations?
   - ☐ A. By preventing the formation of ice.
   - ☐ B. By breaking up ice formations.
   - ☐ C. By allowing only a thin layer of ice to build up.

3. Why are the tubes in deicer boots alternately inflated?
   - ☐ A. Alternate inflation of deicer boot tubes keeps disturbance of the airflow to a minimum.
   - ☐ B. Alternate inflation of deicer boot tubes does not disturb airflow.
   - ☐ C. Alternate inflation of deicer boot tubes relieves the load on the air pump.

4. Carburetor icing may be eliminated by which of the following methods?
   - ☐ A. Alcohol spray and heated induction air.
   - ☐ B. Ethylene glycol spray and heated induction air.
   - ☐ C. Electrically heating air intake, ethylene glycol spray, or alcohol spray.

5. What mixture may be used as a deicing fluid to remove frost from an aircraft surface?
   - ☐ A. Ethylene glycol and isopropyl alcohol.
   - ☐ B. Methyl ethyl ketone and ethylene glycol.
   - ☐ C. Naphtha and isopropyl alcohol.

6. What should be used to melt the ice in a turbine engine if the compressor is immobile because of ice?
   - ☐ A. Deicing fluid.
   - ☐ B. Anti-icing fluid.
   - ☐ C. Hot air.

7. What maintains normal windshield temperature control in an electrically heated windshield system?
   - ☐ A. Thermal overheat switches.
   - ☐ B. Thermistors.
   - ☐ C. Electronic amplifiers.

8. What is the principle of a windshield pneumatic rain removal system?
   - ☐ A. An air blast spreads a liquid rain repellent evenly over the windshield that prevents raindrops from clinging to the glass surface.
   - ☐ B. An air blast forms a barrier that prevents raindrops from striking the windshield surface.
   - ☐ C. A pneumatic rain removal system is simply a mechanical windshield wiper system that is powered by pneumatic system pressure.

9. What controls the inflation sequence in a pneumatic deicer boot system?
   - ☐ A. Shuttle valve.
   - ☐ B. Vacuum pump.
   - ☐ C. Distributor valve.

10. Which of the following is the best means to use when removing wet snow from an aircraft?
    - ☐ A. A brush or a squeegee.
    - ☐ B. Hot air.
    - ☐ C. Warm water.

11. What is one check for proper operation of a pitot/static tube heater after replacement?
    - ☐ A. Ammeter reading.
    - ☐ B. Voltmeter reading.
    - ☐ C. Continuity check of system.

ICE AND RAIN PROTECTION

12. What is the source of pressure for inflating deicer boots on reciprocating engine aircraft?
    - ☐ A. Vane type pump.
    - ☐ B. Gear type pump.
    - ☐ C. Piston type pump.

13. Which of the following regulates the vacuum of the air pump to hold the deicing boots deflated when the pneumatic deicing system is off?
    - ☐ A. Distributor valve.
    - ☐ B. Pressure regulator.
    - ☐ C. Suction relief valve.

14. What may be used to clean deicer boots?
    - ☐ A. Unleaded gasoline or Jet A fuel.
    - ☐ B. Naphtha.
    - ☐ C. Soap and water.

15. Some aircraft are protected against airframe icing by heating the leading edges of the airfoils and intake ducts. When is this type of anti-ice system usually operated during flight?
    - ☐ A. Continuously while the aircraft is in flight.
    - ☐ B. In symmetric cycles during icing conditions to remove ice as it accumulates.
    - ☐ C. Whenever icing conditions are first encountered or expected to occur.

16. Which of the following indications occur during a normal operational check of a pneumatic deicer system?
    - ☐ A. Relatively steady readings on the pressure gauge and fluctuating readings on the vacuum gauge.
    - ☐ B. Fluctuating readings on the pressure gauge and relatively steady readings on the vacuum gauge.
    - ☐ C. Pressure and vacuum gauges will fluctuate as the deicer boots inflate and deflate.

17. What method is usually employed to control the temperature of an anti-icing system using surface combustion heaters?
    - ☐ A. Thermo cycling switches.
    - ☐ B. Thermostats in the cockpit.
    - ☐ C. Heater fuel shutoff valves.

18. What is the purpose of the distributor valve in a deicing system utilizing deicer boots?
    - ☐ A. To equalize the air pressure to the left and right wings.
    - ☐ B. To sequence the deicer boots inflations symmetrically.
    - ☐ C. To distribute anti-icing fluid to the deicer boots.

19. What is the purpose of the oil separator in the pneumatic deicing system?
    - ☐ A. To protect the deicer boots from oil deterioration.
    - ☐ B. To remove oil from air exhausted from the deicer boots.
    - ☐ C. To prevent an accumulation of oil in the vacuum system.

20. Where are the heat sensors located on most aircraft with electrically heated windshields?
    - ☐ A. Embedded in the glass.
    - ☐ B. Attached to the glass.
    - ☐ C. Around the glass.

21. Ice buildup increases _____ and reduces _____.
    - ☐ A. drag, lift
    - ☐ B. lift, drag
    - ☐ C. drag, temperature

22. What type of valve controls the flow of bleed air from the pneumatic system to the wing anti-ice ducts?
    - ☐ A. Bleed air valve.
    - ☐ B. Wing anti-ice valve.
    - ☐ C. Cross feed valve.

ICE AND RAIN PROTECTION

23. Pneumatic deicing systems (boots) are used on _____
    - ☐ A. general aviation aircraft.
    - ☐ B. transport category aircraft.
    - ☐ C. general aviation and transport category aircraft.
    - ☐ D. helicopters.

24. Why is an oil separator necessary in a deicing outfitted with a wet pump?
    - ☐ A. To improve lubrication of the pump.
    - ☐ B. To improve vacuum pressure.
    - ☐ C. To remove the oil from the air.

25. On modern aircraft the deicer boots are _____ to the leading edge of a wing.
    - ☐ A. Riveted with flush rivets.
    - ☐ B. Bolted with rivnuts.
    - ☐ C. Bonded with an adhesive.

Chapter 15, Final Chapter Exam - Ice and Rain Protection

Name: _____ Date: _____

ICE AND RAIN PROTECTION

PAGE LEFT BLANK INTENTIONALLY

CABIN ENVIRONMENTAL CONTROL SYSTEMS

CHAPTER 16

Section A
Study Aid Questions - Fill In The Blanks

1. Oxygen is a _____, _____, and _____ gas at normal atmospheric temperatures and pressures.

2. The words _____ should be marked clearly on any cylinder containing oxygen for aircraft use.

3. Oxygen cylinders are considered empty when the pressure inside drops below _____ psi. This ensures that air containing _____ has not entered the cylinder.

4. When oxygen is delivered only as the user inhales, it is known as a _____ system.

5. There are two types of individual oxygen demand regulators. They are:

    1.   2.

6. The main cause of contamination in an oxygen system is _____.

7. The cabin pressurization system must be capable of maintaining a cabin pressure attitude of _____ or lower regardless of _____.

8. Metal fatigue from repeated _____, and _____ weakens the aircraft structure.

9. There are three typical sources of air used to pressurize reciprocating aircraft. They are:

    1.   2.   3.

10. Aircraft equipped with turbine engines typically use _____ as a source for cabin pressurization.

11. Aircraft cabin pressurization systems work in two different modes of operation. They are:

    1.   2.

12. The flight crew can select and control _____, _____, and _____ on the cabin pressure controller.

13. The cabin pressure controller controls the position of the _____ located normally at the rear of the aircraft.

14. Many transport category aircraft have an outflow valve that operates _____, using signals sent from a remotely located _____ that act as the pressure regulator.

CABIN ENVIRONMENTAL CONTROL SYSTEMS

15. Pressurization safety relieve valves are used to prevent _____ of the cabin.

16. _____ are used to ensure that air pressure outside the aircraft does not exceed cabin air pressure.

17. Aircraft with reciprocating engines often use a _____ cooling system, and turbine powered aircraft use a _____ cooling system.

18. The air cycle cooling system is supplied with air from either _____ or _____.

19. The heart of the air cycle cooling system is the _____, also known as the _____.

20. The duct temperature sensors used in the temperature control system are _____. Their _____ changes as temperature changes.

21. The temperature at which a substance changes from a _____ into a _____ when heat is added is known as the boiling point.

22. R134a refrigerant is filtered and stored under pressure in a reservoir known as _____.

23. Most evaporators are constructed of _____ or _____ tubing coiled into a compact unit.

24. A concern of exhaust shroud heat systems is that _____ could contaminate the cabin.

25. Maintenance of combustion heaters consists of routine items such as _____, checking _____ wear, and ensuring inlets are not plugged.

Section A
True of False

___ 1. Gaseous oxygen systems are used in commercial aircraft and LOX oxygen systems are primarily used in military aircraft.

___ 2. Most oxygen storage cylinders are painted blue, but yellow and white may be used as well.

___ 3. Demand-flow systems are used most frequently by the crew on high performance and air transport category aircraft.

___ 4. A blown out green disk in the side of fuselage indicates that the oxygen supply is low and this should be investigated before flight.

___ 5. The solid chemical oxygen generators used in most airliners are activated automatically by depressurization or manually by a switch operated by the flight crew.

___ 6. Petroleum products such as grease and oil should never be used for oxygen system maintenance because an explosion could be the result.

CABIN ENVIRONMENTAL CONTROL SYSTEMS

True of False (continued)

_____ 7. The cabin pressurization system must maintain the cabin pressure altitude below 10,000 ft.

_____ 8. Metal fatigue can result from repeated pressurization cycles and can weaken the airframe structure.

_____ 9. Superchargers are the common source of pressurization on modern reciprocating engine aircraft.

_____ 10. Turbochargers are driven by a shaft or a drive belt.

_____ 11. Large turbine powered aircraft use bleed air from the engine compressor section as a source of air for cabin pressurization.

_____ 12. The isobaric control mode of a cabin pressurization system controls cabin pressure to maintain a constant pressure between the air pressure outside the cabin and the ambient air pressure.

_____ 13. Small aircraft often use a pneumatically controlled outflow valve while transport category aircraft use electrically/electronically controlled outflow valves.

_____ 14. Pressurization safety relieve valves are used to prevent negative cabin pressure.

_____ 15. Many pack valves used in air conditioning systems are electrically controlled and pneumatically operated.

_____ 16. The primary heat exchanger is cooled by an electric fan during stationary ground operations and ram air is used in flight.

_____ 17. The water separator has a fiberglass bag (sock) that condenses and coalesces the mist into larger water droplets. Gravity will drain the water droplets from the water separator.

_____ 18. The function of the refrigeration by-pass valve is to regulate the temperature of the air cycle machine so it does not freeze when passing through the water separator.

_____ 19. A vapor cycle air conditioning system is an open system in which a refrigerant is circulated through tubing and a variety of components.

_____ 20. Most modern vapor cycle cooling systems on aircraft use R12 refrigerant which has replaced the R134a refrigerant.

_____ 21. During a feel test components and lines in the high side (from the compressor to the expansion valve) should warm or hot to the touch.

_____ 22. During a feel test low side lines and the evaporator should be warm.

_____ 23. The charging capacity of a vapor cycle air conditioning system is measured by weight.

_____ 24. Most single-engine light aircraft use a bleed air system to heat the cabin.

_____ 25. The fuel for the combustion heater is drawn from a dedicated small fuel tank inside the cabin.

Chapter 16, Section A - Cabin Environmental Control Systems

Name:_____ Date:_____

8083-31B-ATB Airframe Workbook

CABIN ENVIRONMENTAL CONTROL SYSTEMS

PAGE LEFT BLANK INTENTIONALLY

CABIN ENVIRONMENTAL CONTROL SYSTEMS

Section B
Knowledge Application Questions

1. What component in the pressurization system is the principal control of a pressurization system?

2. What source of air supply is used by most turbine-powered aircraft for pressurization?

3. What pressurization control unit will change the position of an outflow valve?

4. On reciprocating engine aircraft, what are some methods of supplying heat to the cabin?

5. What is the function of ventilating air in a combustion heater?

6. What are the typical components used in an air cycle cooling system?

7. What causes a temperature drop in an air cycle cooling system?

8. Describe how a water separator in an air cycle cooling system removes moisture from the air?

9. Describe the theory of operation of a vapor cycle cooling system illustrated in Airframe Handbook Figure 16-74?

CABIN ENVIRONMENTAL CONTROL SYSTEMS

10. Describe the theory of operation of an air cycle cooling system illustrated in textbook Figure 16-63.

11. What are the main components in a vapor cycle cooling system?

12. How does a continuous-flow oxygen system operate?

13. What must be accomplished if an oxygen system has been open to atmosphere for 2 hours or more?

14. What is used to purge oxygen lines of moisture?

15. What type of oxygen must be used in aircraft?

16. Why is oil added to a vapor cycle Freon system?

17. What safety precautions should be observed when servicing oxygen systems?

18. What sources of air are used by pressurized aircraft with a reciprocating engine?

19. What is the main advantage of using LOX systems?

CABIN ENVIRONMENTAL CONTROL SYSTEMS

20. What kind of adjustments can be made on a pressure controller?

21. Explain the need for regular and careful inspections of exhaust heating systems.

22. What fuel is used in a combustion heater?

23. Why is a dryer essential in a vapor-cycle system?

24. Why is aircraft pressurization necessary?

25. What are the sources of aircraft-pressurization air pressure?

26. What method is used by some turbine-powered aircraft for pressurization?

27. Explain the need for limiting the pressure differential between the inside of the cabin and the outside.

28. What is the principal control of a pressurization system?

29. What is the purpose of a negative pressure-relief valve?

CABIN ENVIRONMENTAL CONTROL SYSTEMS

30. What are the functions of the automatic and manual controllers in the pressurization system?

Chapter 16, Section B - Cabin Environmental Control Systems

Name: _____ Date: _____

CABIN ENVIRONMENTAL CONTROL SYSTEMS

Section C
Final Chapter Exam

1. The purpose of the dump valve in a pressurized aircraft is to relieve _____
   - ☐ A. all positive pressure from the cabin.
   - ☐ B. a negative pressure differential.
   - ☐ C. pressure in excess of the maximum differential.

2. The basic air cycle cooling system consists of _____
   - ☐ A. a source of compressed air, heat exchangers, and an air cycle machine.
   - ☐ B. heaters, coolers, and compressors.
   - ☐ C. ram air source, compressors, and engine bleeds.

3. Frost or ice buildup on a vapor cycle cooling system evaporator would most likely be caused by _____
   - ☐ A. the mixing valve sticking closed.
   - ☐ B. moisture in the evaporator.
   - ☐ C. inadequate airflow through the evaporator.

4. What component in a vapor cycle cooling system would most likely be at fault if a system would not take a Freon charge?
   - ☐ A. Expansion valve.
   - ☐ B. Condenser.
   - ☐ C. Receiver dryer.

5. What controls the operation of the cabin pressure regulator?
   - ☐ A. Cabin altitude.
   - ☐ B. Bleed air pressure.
   - ☐ C. Compression air pressure.

6. The cabin pressure of an aircraft in flight is maintained at the selected altitude by _____
   - ☐ A. controlling the air inflow rate.
   - ☐ B. inflating door seals and recirculating conditioned cabin air.
   - ☐ C. controlling the rate at which air leaves the cabin.

7. What is ventilating air used for on a combustion heater?
   - ☐ A. Provides combustion air for ground blower.
   - ☐ B. Carries heat to the places where needed.
   - ☐ C. Provides air required to support the flame.

8. At which component in an air cycle cooling system does air undergo a pressure and temperature drop?
   - ☐ A. Expansion turbine.
   - ☐ B. Primary heat exchanger.
   - ☐ C. Refrigeration bypass valve.

9. How often should standard weight high pressure oxygen cylinders be hydrostatically tested?
   - ☐ A. Every 5 years.
   - ☐ B. Every 4 years.
   - ☐ C. Every 3 years.

10. In an operating vapor cycle cooling system, if the two lines connected to the expansion valve are essentially the same temperature, what does this indicate?
    - ☐ A. The system is functioning normally.
    - ☐ B. The expansion valve is not metering Freon properly.
    - ☐ C. The compressor is pumping too much refrigerant.

11. In the diluter demand oxygen regulator, when does the demand valve operate?
    - ☐ A. When the diluter control is set at normal.
    - ☐ B. When the user demands 100 percent oxygen.
    - ☐ C. When the user breathes.

CABIN ENVIRONMENTAL CONTROL SYSTEMS

12. If oxygen bottle pressure is allowed to drop below a specified minimum, it may cause _____
    - ☐ A. the pressure reducer to fail.
    - ☐ B. the automatic altitude control valve to open.
    - ☐ C. moisture to collect in the bottle.

13. In a high-pressure oxygen system, if the pressure reducer fails, what prevents high pressure oxygen from entering the system downstream?
    - ☐ A. Check valve.
    - ☐ B. Pressure relief valve.
    - ☐ C. Manifold control valve.

14. What is the condition of the refrigerant as it leaves the condenser of a vapor cycle cooling system?
    - ☐ A. Low pressure liquid.
    - ☐ B. High pressure liquid.
    - ☐ C. High pressure vapor.

15. What is the condition of the refrigerant as it leaves the evaporator of a vapor cycle cooling system?
    - ☐ A. Low pressure liquid.
    - ☐ B. Low pressure vapor.
    - ☐ C. High pressure vapor.

16. The primary difference between aviation breathing oxygen and other types of commercially available compressed oxygen is that _____
    - ☐ A. the other types are usually somewhat less than 99.5 percent pure oxygen.
    - ☐ B. aviation breathing oxygen has had all the water vapor removed.
    - ☐ C. aviation breathing oxygen has a higher percentage of water vapor to help prevent drying of a person's breathing passages and possible dehydration.

17. In a gaseous oxygen system, which of the following are vented to blow out plugs in the fuselage skin?
    - ☐ A. Pressure relief valves.
    - ☐ B. Filler shutoff valves.
    - ☐ C. Pressure reducer valves.

18. What part of a pressurization system prevents cabin altitude from becoming higher than airplane altitude?
    - ☐ A. Cabin rate of descent control.
    - ☐ B. Negative pressure relief valve.
    - ☐ C. Positive pressure relief valve.

19. The cabin pressure control setting has a direct influence upon the _____
    - ☐ A. outflow valve opening.
    - ☐ B. pneumatic system pressure.
    - ☐ C. onflow valve opening.

20. If the cabin rate of climb is too great, the control should be adjusted to cause the _____
    - ☐ A. outflow valve to close slower.
    - ☐ B. outflow valve to close faster.
    - ☐ C. cabin compressor speed to decrease.

21. The main cause of contamination in gaseous oxygen systems is _____
    - ☐ A. moisture.
    - ☐ B. dust and other airborne particulates.
    - ☐ C. other atmospheric gases.

22. What may be used as a lubricant on oxygen system tapered pipe thread connections?
    - ☐ A. Silicone dielectric compound.
    - ☐ B. Glycerin.
    - ☐ C. Teflon tape.

CABIN ENVIRONMENTAL CONTROL SYSTEMS

23. Which best describes cabin differential pressure?
    - ☐ A. Difference between cabin flight altitude pressure and Mean Sea Level pressure.
    - ☐ B. Difference between the ambient and internal air pressure.
    - ☐ C. Difference between cabin pressure controller setting and actual cabin pressure.

24. Regarding the statements below, which is true?
    01. Usually bleed air from a gas-turbine engine compressor can be safely used for cabin pressurization.
    02. Independent cabin condition air machines (air cycle machine) can be powered by bleed air from an aircraft turbine engine compressor.
    - ☐ A. Only No. 01 is true.
    - ☐ B. Only No. 02 is true.
    - ☐ C. Both No. 01 and No. 02 are true.

25. The cabin pressurization modes of operation are _____
    - ☐ A. isobaric, differential, and maximum differential.
    - ☐ B. differential, unpressurized, and isobaric.
    - ☐ C. ambient, unpressurized, and isobaric.

Chapter 16, Final Chapter Exam - Cabin Environmental Control Systems

Name:_____ Date:_____

CABIN ENVIRONMENTAL CONTROL SYSTEMS

PAGE LEFT BLANK INTENTIONALLY

FIRE PROTECTION SYSTEMS

CHAPTER 17

Section A
Study Aid Questions - Fill In The Blanks

1. Because fire is one of the most dangerous threats to an aircraft, the potential fire zones of modern multiengine aircraft are protected by _____ system.

2. Three detector systems in common use are the _____, _____, and _____.

3. A thermocouple depends on the _____ and will not give a warning when an engine _____ overheats or a short circuit develops.

4. The thermocouple is constructed of two dissimilar metals such _____ and _____.

5. Two widely used types of continuous-loop systems are _____ type detectors such as the Kidde and the Fenwal systems, and the pneumatic pressure detector such as the _____ system.

6. The Kidde continuous-loop system can supply _____ data to the airplane condition monitoring function of the Aircraft In-flight Monitoring System.

7. Dual loop systems use a _____ logic to increase system reliability.

8. Lindberg systems are also know as _____ and _____.

9. A smoke detection system monitors _____, _____, and baggage compartments for the presence of _____, which is indicative of fire condition.

10. Optical sensors often referred to as _____.

11. Carbon monoxide detectors are installed in the cockpit of aircraft powered by _____ engines to detect for _____ gas which can enter the cockpit through _____ malfunctions.

12. Class A type fires are best controlled with _____ by cooling the material below its _____ temperature and soaking the material to prevent re-ignition.

13. _____ is not recommended for hand-held extinguishers for internal aircraft use.

14. _____ systems use open-end tubes to deliver a quantity of extinguishing agent in _____ seconds.

15. Fire extinguisher containers (HRD bottles) store a _____ halogenated extinguishing agent and pressurized _____ and are normally manufactured from stainless steel.

FIRE PROTECTION SYSTEMS

Section A
True of False

_____ 1. A fire protection system on most aircraft consists of a fire detection and a fire extinguishing system.

_____ 2. Smoke detectors are not used in cargo and baggage compartments.

_____ 3. Class D fires are fires involving energized electrical equipment where the use of an extinguishing media that is electrically nonconductive is important.

_____ 4. Thermal switches are pressure-sensitive units that complete electrical circuits at a certain temperature.

_____ 5. Transport aircraft almost exclusively use continuous thermal sensing elements for power plant and wheel well protection.

_____ 6. Halocarbon clean agents or water are used on a Class D fire.

_____ 7. The Fenwal system uses a slender Inconel tube packed with thermally sensitive eutectic salt and a nickel wire center conductor.

_____ 8. When the fire or overheat condition is gone, the resistance of the core material in the Kidde system will increase to the reset point and the flight deck indications go away.

_____ 9. Pneumatic continuous loop systems are used for engine fire detection of reciprocating type aircraft and have the same function as the Kidde system; however they work on a different principle.

_____ 10. The Lindberg fire/overheat detector's sensor tube also contains a hydrogen filled core material.

Chapter 17, Section A - Fire Protection Systems

Name:_____ Date:_____

FIRE PROTECTION SYSTEMS

Section B
Knowledge Application Questions

1. Name five typical zones on aircraft that have a fixed fire detection and/or fire extinguisher system?

   1.   3.   5.

   2.   4.

2. What types of systems are used to detect fires in reciprocating engine and small turboprop aircraft?

3. What types of systems are used to detect fire in turbine engine fire protection systems?

4. Name three types of continuous loop fire detection systems.

   1.   2.   3.

5. What are the advantages of using Support tube mounted sensing elements?

6. What type of fire detection and extinguishing systems are controlled by advanced detection system circuitry?

7. What type of extinguishing agents are used for a class A, B, and C fire?

8. Transport aircraft have fixed fire extinguishing systems installed in _____

9. What is installed in the outlet of the discharge valve?

FIRE PROTECTION SYSTEMS

10. What is the function of the cartridge (squib) that is installed in the discharge valve?

11. What is the purpose of the Yellow disk discharge indicator?

12. Which type of fire-detection system is termed a rate-of-rise detection system?

13. What is a Class A cargo or baggage compartment?

14. What is the difference between a Class A and a Class B cargo and baggage compartment?

15. What indications will occur in the cockpit if there is smoke in a cargo compartment?

Figure 17-1.

FIRE PROTECTION SYSTEMS

16. What could be the results of kinks and sharp bends in the sensing element?

17. Using the pressure chart (Figure 17-1) below. What is the minimum pressure when the temperature is 70°F?

18. Describe the theory of operation of a spot detector and a thermocouple system.

19. How is a thermocouple fire warning system different from a thermal switch system?

20. How are overheat and fire warning systems tested for operational capability?

21. What indications may be caused by kinks and sharp bends in sensing elements of a fire

22. How are sensors protected from vibration, wear, and damage?

23. What are two types of installed fire extinguishing systems?

24. What gas is usually employed to expel the extinguishing agent from a container?

25. To what pressure is a container usually charged?

FIRE PROTECTION SYSTEMS

26. How is the service life of a discharge cartridge calculated?

27. What is used to indicate that a fire-extinguishing agent bottle has discharged thermally?

28. What is the purpose of the yellow disk in a fire extinguisher system?

29. What are two classifications of fire-extinguishing systems?

30. What type of extinguishing agent should be used for electrical fires?

Chapter 17, Section B - Fire Protection Systems

Name:_____ Date:_____

FIRE PROTECTION SYSTEMS

Section C
Final Chapter Exam

1. A squib, as used in a fire protection system is a _____
   - ☐ A. temperature sensing device.
   - ☐ B. device for causing the fire extinguishing agent to be released.
   - ☐ C. probe used for installing frangible disks in extinguisher bottles.

2. When used in fire detection systems having a single indicator light, thermal switches are wired in _____
   - ☐ A. parallel with each other and in series with the light.
   - ☐ B. series with each other and the light.
   - ☐ C. series with each other and parallel with the light.

3. If the temperature of the Kidde continuous loop core _____ the electrical resistance to ground _____
   - ☐ A. Increases; decreases.
   - ☐ B. Decreases; decreases.
   - ☐ C. Decreases; increases.

CONTAINER PRESSURE VERSUS TEMPERATURE		
Temperature °F	Container Pressure (psi)	
	Minimum	Maximum
-40	60	145
-30	83	165
-20	105	188
-10	125	210
0	145	230
10	167	252
20	188	275
30	209	295
40	230	317
50	255	342
60	284	370
70	319	405
80	356	443
90	395	483
100	438	523

4. Referring to the chart above, determine the maximum pressure (psi) on an 80°F day.
   - ☐ A. 443 psi
   - ☐ B. 405 psi
   - ☐ C. 356 psi

5. What method is used to detect the thermal discharge of a built-in fire extinguisher system?
   - ☐ A. A discoloring of the yellow plastic disk in the thermal discharge line.
   - ☐ B. A rupture of the red plastic disk in the thermal discharge line.
   - ☐ C. The thermal plug missing from the side of the bottle.

6. The thermal switches of a bimetallic thermal switch type fire detection system are heat sensitive units that complete circuits at a certain temperature. They are connected in _____
   - ☐ A. parallel with each other, and in parallel with the indicator lights.
   - ☐ B. parallel with each other, but in series with the indicator lights.
   - ☐ C. series with each other, but in parallel with the indicator lights.

FIRE PROTECTION SYSTEMS

7. Lindberg fire detection systems use a loop system that is filled with a _____ and use a _____ to actuate the control circuitry.
   - ☐ A. thermistor material; pressure diaphragm
   - ☐ B. gas; thermocouple
   - ☐ C. gas; pressure diaphragm

8. On a periodic check of fire extinguisher containers, the pressure was not between minimum and maximum limits. What procedure should be followed?
   - ☐ A. Release pressure if above limits.
   - ☐ B. Replace the extinguisher container.
   - ☐ C. Increase pressure if below limits.

9. In some fire extinguishing systems, evidence that the system has been intentionally discharged is indicated by the absence of a _____
   - ☐ A. red disk on the side of the fuselage.
   - ☐ B. green disk on the side of the fuselage.
   - ☐ C. yellow disk on the side of the fuselage.

10. The thermocouple fire warning system is activated by a _____
    - ☐ A. certain temperature.
    - ☐ B. core resistance drop.
    - ☐ C. rate of temperature rise.

11. Maintenance of fire detection systems includes the _____
    - ☐ A. repair of damaged sensing elements.
    - ☐ B. removal of excessive loop or element material.
    - ☐ C. replacement of damaged sensing elements.

12. A carbon dioxide (CO_2) hand held fire extinguisher may be used on an electrical fire if the _____
    - ☐ A. horn is nonmetallic.
    - ☐ B. handle is insulated.
    - ☐ C. horn is nonmagnetic.

13. Which fire extinguishing agent is considered to be the least toxic?
    - ☐ A. Carbon dioxide.
    - ☐ B. Bromotrifluoromethane (Halon 1301).
    - ☐ C. Bromochloromethane (Halon 1011).

14. Which fire detection system measures temperature rise compared to a reference temperature?
    - ☐ A. Fenwal continuous loop.
    - ☐ B. Lindberg continuous element.
    - ☐ C. Thermocouple.

15. In what area of an aircraft would you find a carbon monoxide detector?
    - ☐ A. Surface combustion heater compartment.
    - ☐ B. Cockpit and/or cabin.
    - ☐ C. Engine and/or nacelle.

16. What occurs when a visual smoke detector is activated?
    - ☐ A. A warning bell within the indicator alarms automatically.
    - ☐ B. A lamp within the indicator illuminates automatically.
    - ☐ C. The test lamp illuminates and an alarm is provided automatically.

17. The types of fire extinguishing agents for aircraft interior fires are _____
    - ☐ A. water, carbon dioxide, dry chemical, and halogenated hydrocarbons.
    - ☐ B. water, dry chemical, methyl bromide, and chlorobromomethane.
    - ☐ C. water, carbon tetrachloride, carbon dioxide, and dry chemical.

FIRE PROTECTION SYSTEMS

18. When air samples contain carbon monoxide, portable carbon monoxide detectors containing yellow silica gel will turn which color?
    - ☐ A. Blue.
    - ☐ B. Green.
    - ☐ C. Red.

19. Smoke detection instruments are classified by their method of _____
    - ☐ A. construction.
    - ☐ B. maintenance.
    - ☐ C. detection.

20. Smoke in the cargo and/or baggage compartment of an aircraft is commonly detected by which instrument?
    - ☐ A. Chemical reactor.
    - ☐ B. Photoelectric cell.
    - ☐ C. Sniffer.

21. A contaminated carbon monoxide portable test unit would be returned to service by _____
    - ☐ A. heating the indicating element to 300°F to reactivate the chemical.
    - ☐ B. installing a new indicating element.
    - ☐ C. evacuating the indicating element with CO_2.

22. A thermocouple in a fire detection system causes the warning system to operate because _____
    - ☐ A. it generates a small current when heated.
    - ☐ B. heat decreases its electrical resistance.
    - ☐ C. it expands when heated and forms a ground for the warning system.

23. The proper fire extinguishing agent to use on an aircraft brake fire is _____
    - ☐ A. water.
    - ☐ B. carbon dioxide.
    - ☐ C. dry powder chemical.

24. Why does the Fenwal fire detection system use spot detectors wired parallel between two separate circuits?
    - ☐ A. A control unit is used to isolate the bad system in case of malfunction.
    - ☐ B. This installation is equal to two systems: a main system and a reserve system.
    - ☐ C. A short may exist in either circuit without causing a false fire warning.

25. A fire extinguisher container can be checked to determine its charge by _____
    - ☐ A. attaching a remote pressure gauge.
    - ☐ B. weighing the container and its contents.
    - ☐ C. a hydrostatic test.

Chapter 17, Final Chapter Exam - Fire Protection Systems

Name: _____ Date: _____

FIRE PROTECTION SYSTEMS

PAGE LEFT BLANK INTENTIONALLY

ANSWERS

CHAPTER 1
Aircraft Structures

Section A - Fill in the Blanks
1. structural member
2. torsion, shear
3. pounds per square inch, psi
4. full cantilever
5. spanwise
6. longerons
7. web, cap
8. firewall, engine
9. regulate engine temperature
10. lateral, longitudinal, and directional
11. flutter
12. left
13. lateral or horizontal
14. Right
15. fowler
16. AOA or angle of attack
17. spoilers
18. zero station
19. stainless steel
20. up and down, back and forth

Section A - True or False
1. False - Wing Spar
2. False - Tension
3. True
4. False - Stringers
5. False - Skin Carries Load
6. True
7. False - Ribs Forward of Front Spar Used For Shaping and Strengthening Leading Edge
8. True
9. True
10. False - Electrical and Hydraulic Power
11. False - Wing Sealed with Fuel Resistant Sealing
12. True
13. False - Installed and Operate Dependently
14. False - Winglets
15. False - Conventional and Tailwheel
16. True
17. True
18. False - Tilting the Rotor
19. False - Flap
20. False - Opposite Direction of Rotation

Section B - Knowledge Application
1. Rotors are rotating wings as opposed to propellers and rotating airfoils of an engine.
2. The degree of deformation of a material.
3. The part is shortened or compressed on the inside of the bend and stretched on the outside of the bend. This is a combination of compression and tension stress.
4. They must be streamlined to meet aerodynamic requirements to reduce drag or direct airflow.
5. Members such as beams, struts, bars, and longerons covered with fabric.
6. Maintaining the proper amount of strength while keeping the weight within the allowable limits
7. Monocoque fuselages have heavy structural members located at intervals with no other bracing members, requiring the skin to carry the primary loads. Semimonocoque type fuselage uses longerons as longitudinal reinforcements that help support the skin.
8. Metal fatigue is caused by cycling from pressurized to unpressurized and back during each flight as well as withstanding the pressure differential inflight.
9. Jury struts subdue strut movement and oscillation on struts that are attached to the wings at a great distance from the fuselage. They are vertical support structures that are attached to the wing and strut.
10. They are the principal structural member and they support all distributed loads as well as concentrated weights (i.e., fuselage, landing gear, engines, etc.).
11. They are located entirely forward of the front spar and they are used to shape and strengthen the wing leading edge. They do not span the entire wing chord.
12. They are streamlined and house the engine and its components. They can sometimes be designed to house the landing gear. All nacelles incorporate a firewall to isolate the engine from the rest of the airframe. They have cowlings which cover areas that can be easily accessed when detached.
13. Lateral-elevators, longitudinal-ailerons, vertical-rudder.
14. Camber and lift are increased.
15. Slots direct air over the upper surface of the wing during high angles of attack. They lower stall speed and provide control during slow flight. Slots are located on the outer leading edge of the wing forward of the ailerons.
16. Typically linked directly to the control surface so they move automatically when the control surface moves. Balance tabs aide the pilot in overcoming the force needed to move the control surface.
17. Allows for greater clearance between the propeller, which were longer back then, and loose debris when operating on unpaved runway.
18. The two main wheels are forward of the center of gravity while the tail is aft. If the aircraft swerves on landing the tail can swing out pulling the center of gravity aft of the main wheels allowing the tail to freely pivot.
19. As the plane of rotation of the rotor blade tilts the advancing blade has a greater relative windspeed compared to the retreating blade. This causes a greater amount of lift being developed on the advancing blade resulting in the blade flapping up. The opposite occurs on the retreating side causing the blade to flap down.
20. Stands for "no tail rotor" because it has an engine driven adjustable fan located in the tail boom. As the speed of the main rotor changes, the speed of the NOTAR fan changes as well. Air is vented out of two long slots on the right side of the tail to counteract the torque produced by the main rotor.

8083-31B-ATB Airframe Workbook

ANSWERS

CHAPTER 2
Aerodynamics, Aircraft Assembly, and Rigging

Section A - Fill in the Blanks
1. Force, dyne
2. Hg or inches of mercury, barometer
3. Increases, increases, increases
4. Inversely, directly
5. First, inertia
6. Increase
7. upper surface
8. AOA or angle of attack
9. Longitudinal
10. Fluid, pressure
11. High, low, outward, vortex
12. Static
13. Ailerons, elevator, rudder
14. Free-spinning, upward
15. Down
16. Left, all
17. Dissymmetry
18. Clutch
19. Right, left
20. "Go" and "no-go"
21. Fairleads, 3°
22. Turnbuckle, left-hand
23. Position or angle, wing tips
24. Dihedral, incidence
25. Double-twist, single-wire

Section A - True or False
1. True
2. True
3. False - Faster At Higher Altitude
4. False - Inversely
5. True
6. True
7. False - Lift To Drag Ratio
8. False - Drag, Not Weight
9. True
10. False - Center Of Gravity
11. False - Vertical Axis
12. True
13. False - Wing Fences
14. True
15. True
16. False - Weight Added Fore or Aft of Hinges
17. False - Manufacturer Provides Instructions for Fabrication
18. True
19. False - Issued by FAA
20. False - Flexible and Used for Pulleys
21. False - Not Used
22. True
23. True
24. True
25. False - Never Reused

Section B - Knowledge Application
1. It is a substance that has the ability to flow or assume the shape of the container in which it is enclosed.
2. Atmospheric pressure is the force exerted against the earth's surface by the weight of the air above that surface. It is measured using a barometer in "Hg.
3. Density varies in direct proportion with pressure and inversely with temperature.
4. Absolute - the weight of water vapor in a unit volume of air; Relative - the ratio (%) of the moisture actually in the air to the moisture it would hold if it were saturated at the same temperature and pressure.
5. The law of action and reaction states that for every action (force) there is an equal and opposite reaction (force).
6. The top part of the wing has a greater curvature than the bottom. This requires the air above the wing to travel farther than the bottom. The air therefore, has a greater velocity and a decreased pressure. The pressure differential creates lift. The high pressure on the bottom of the wing tries to equalize by rising to the low pressure area.
7. There is an area of negative pressure behind the resultant force when AOA is 0°. As AOA increases towards its critical point, the resultant force moves forward. Once critical angle is reached the resultant force falls rapidly until the wing stalls.
8. Drag is the resistance of the air to an object moving through it. There are 3 forms of drag: Parasite drag occurs when an exposed object offers resistance to the air. Profile drag is the parasite drag of the airfoil. Induced drag occurs as lift is created and the air flow spillage over the wing tip creates a vortex. This vortex constitutes induced drag.
9. Control is the pilot action of moving the flight controls, providing the aerodynamic force that induces the aircraft to follow a desired flight path. Controllability means that the aircraft responds easily and promptly to movement of the flight controls.
10. Sharp disturbances generate shock waves that affect lift and drag as well as airflow downstream of the shockwave. A cone of pressure which moves outward and rearward from the shockwave. Also, the energy of the object moving excites the chemical bonds of the oxygen and nitrogen.
11. Each blade can move back and forth in plane, lead and lag; and flap up and down through a hinge independent of the other blades.
12. As the engine turns the main rotor in a counterclockwise direction, the helicopter fuselage tends to turn the opposite direction. The action of the main rotor blade creates an equal and opposite force that turns the fuselage clockwise.
13. It is a mechanical connection between the collective lever and engine throttle. When the collective lever is raised, power increases and when lowered, power is decreased. This system maintains RPM close to the desired value.
14. Loose elevator linkage at swash plate horn, loose elevator, or tail rotor balance and track.
15. The gas producer (compressor turbine) is essentially disconnected from the power turbine. When the engine is started, there is little resistance from the power turbine allowing the gas turbine to accelerate to normal

ANSWERS

idle without the transmission load dragging it down.
16. Pulleys are used to guide cables and change cable direction. Pulley guards prevent jamming or the cable slipping off when slackened due to temperature changes.
17. Positioning the flight controls in the neutral position and locking them in place. Adjusting the cable tension and maintaining control surface neutral. Adjusting the control stops to the aircraft manufacturer's specifications.
18. To make minor adjustments in cable length and for adjusting cable tension.
19. Trim tab systems. As the trim tab control moves, the cable drum winds or unwinds to actuate the trim tab cables.
20. Annual, 100-hour inspection, progressive.

CHAPTER 3
Aircraft Fabric Covering

Section A - Fill in the Blanks
1. Cotton, sag, doping or nitrate doping
2. 5-10
3. Polyester
4. Pinking shears, unraveling
5. Unairworthy
6. One-time
7. UV light
8. Retarder
9. Fasteners, airflow
10. Organic
11. Weight, stresses
12. Rejuvenator, airworthy
13. Exposed, 1.25 or 1-1/4"
14. Blanket, precut or pre-sewn
15. Temperature, humidity
16. Volume, pressure
17. Durability, appearance
18. Propeller wash, one rib
19. Inspection or maintenance, inspection
20. Patches, strut

Section A - True or False
1. False - Along the length of fabric.
2. True
3. False - FAA issued.
4. True
5. False - Different thread.
6. True
7. True
8. True
9. False - All coatings should be removed.
10. False - Not an FAA approved method.
11. True
12. True
13. True
14. True
15. False - Dope or Glue
16. True
17. False - Skipping from one end to the other and the middle.
18. True
19. False - The Widest is 4"
20. True

Section B - Knowledge Application
1. They created a system of combining nitrate dope and butyrate dope. The fabric was first coated with nitrate dope for adhesion and protective qualities and then butyrate dope was added reducing the overall flammability.
2. Appendix A states that changing parts of an aircraft wing, tail surface, or fuselage when not listed in the aircraft specifications issued by the FAA is a major alteration and requires a Form 337.
3. It is a self-adhesive cloth tape that is used on sharp protrusions, rib caps, metal seams, and other areas to provide a smoother surface to keep fabric from being torn.
4. The blanket method uses multiple flat sections of fabric trimmed and attached to the airframe. Each aircraft is considered differently to determine size and layout of the blankets but it is typical for a small blanket to be cut for each small surface. Fabric is adhered to the airframe using approved adhesive, and specific manufacturer's instructions.
5. Eye protection, respirator, skin protection, and ventilation.
6. A sheet of felt or polyester padding may be used before the fabric is applied. Approved padding ensures compatibility with the adhesives and first coating of the covering process.
7. Fabric is shrunk in stages, using the lower temperature first. The first shrink removes wrinkles and excess fabric. The final shrinkage gives the desired tautness. Fabric should be shrunk by skipping from one end to the other and then the middle to achieve uniform tautness.
8. Drain grommets allows for an escape of rain water and condensation from under the fabric. They are located at the lowest part of each structural area and each rib bay of the wings. Specific locations of each drain grommet can be found in the AC-43.13 or STC.
9. Chordwise tape is applied first followed by spanwise tape.
10. It is a coat used in some approved covering processes that combines the sealer and fill coats into one. They surround and seal the fabric fibers, provide a good adhesion for following coats, and have UV blocking agents.
11. Polyester fabric coverings are the standard. Cotton and linen used to be used on United States certificated aircraft but its use has ceased.
12. Linen and cotton, were the original fabrics used for covering airframes, but their tendency to sag left the aircraft structure exposed to the elements. These materials have been replaced by polyester.
13. STC-Approved Covering Materials. There is a wide selection of STC-approved covering materials available which utilize synthetic fabric falling within the generic class "Polyester" and may vary in characteristics. Difference in the fabric may be denier, tenacity, thread

ANSWERS

count, weight, shrink, tension, and weave style. Fiberglass is another material that is approved to cover aircraft.
14. In general, an aircraft is certified with a certain fabric based on its wing loading and it's never exceed speed (VNE). The higher the wing loading and VNE, the stronger the fabric must be. On aircraft with wing loading of 9 pounds per square foot and over, or a VNE of 160 miles per hour (mph) or higher, fabric equaling or exceeding the strength of Grade A cotton is required. This means the new fabric breaking strength must be at least 80 pounds and the minimum fabric breaking strength at which the aircraft becomes unairworthy is 56 pounds.
15. Recover or repair aircraft with a fabric of equal quality and strength to that used by the original aircraft manufacturer. It is recommended that fabric conforming to TSO-C15d or TSO-C14b be used to recover aircraft originally covered with lower strength fabric conforming to AMS 3802, current edition.
16. An edge of cloth woven to prevent raveling. The naturally bound edge of a length of fabric. The selvage is where the fill fibers turn around and go back through the warp fibers during the weaving process.
17. Reinforcing tape is most commonly used on rib caps after the fabric covering is installed to protect and strengthen the area for attaching the fabric to the ribs.
18. Grommets are installed where it is necessary to reinforce holes in textile materials used for drainage, lacing, or inspection.
19. The sleeve has been sewed together on a sewing machine, so only a small portion of the material must be closed by hand sewing or a doped seam.
20. Use the chart in AC 43.13-1B.
21. Modified seine knots.
22. To soften and penetrate old dope finishes.
23. The strength of the fabric is based on its tensile strength. Normal testing techniques involve the use of a Seyboth or Maule "punch" tester or when results are marginal, a laboratory test is needed.
24. 30 percent of the original fabric strength. Fabric is considered to be airworthy until it deteriorates to a breaking strength less than 70 percent of the strength of the new fabric required for the aircraft.
25. Fiberglass.

CHAPTER 4
Aircraft Metal Structural Repair

Section A - Fill in the Blanks
1. strong, cracks
2. shear, torsion
3. parallel, three
4. bearing, shear
5. parallel, double-cut
6. shape, half-round
7. pneumatic, electric
8. stops, underlying
9. bends
10. press, complex
11. feed, curvature

12. deburr, stretching
13. V-blocks, flanges
14. thickness, temper
15. K-factor, 90°
16. relief holes, tangent
17. excellent, feed
18. load
19. manufacturing, conventional
20. bulbed, locking (foil)
21. regulated, torque
22. aluminum, clearance
23. sleeves, protruding
24. less, thickest
25. pitch, adjacent
26. knife-edge, enlarging
27. perpendicular, weight
28. spar, strength
29. rivet gage
30. hot, flow

Section B - Knowledge Application

1-1. D	1-5. A	1-9. E
1-2. C	1-6. B	1-10. C
1-3. F	1-7. A	1-11. B
1-4. E	1-8. F	

2-1. L	2-7. E	2-13. M
2-2. C	2-8. O	2-14. R
2-3. I	2-9. G	2-15. B
2-4. Q	2-10. D	2-16. H
2-5. F	2-11. P	2-17. N
2-6. A	2-12. J	2-18. K

3-1. D	3-4. G	3-7. E
3-2. F	3-5. A	3-8. H
3-3. B	3-6. I	3-9. C

4-1. C	4-4. D	4-7. F
4-2. A	4-5. G	
4-3. E	4-6. B	

5-1. E	5-4. F	
5-2. A	5-5. B	
5-3. C	5-6. D	

6-1. H	6-7. F	6-13. J
6-2. L	6-8. A	6-14. G
6-3. D	6-9. K	6-15. M
6-4. P	6-10. B	6-16. C
6-5. I	6-11. O	
6-6. N	6-12. E	

7-1. F	7-4. A	
7-2. B	7-5. D	
7-3. E	7-6. C	

8-1. B	8-6. C	8-11. E
8-2. E	8-7. F	8-12. B
8-3. A	8-8. F	8-13. A
8-4. D	8-9. C	
8-5. G	8-10. G	

ANSWERS

9-1. 2D
9-2. 2D + 1/16"
9-3. 2.5D
9-4. 2.5D + 1/16"

10-1. 3D
10-2. 3D + 1/16"
10-3. 4D
10-4. 4D + 1/16"
10-5. 3.5D
10-6. 3.5D + 1/16"
10-7. 4.5D
10-8. 4.5D + 1/16"

11. It is drawn up into the rivet shank forming a plug in the hollow center of the rivet and continues until the excess portion of the stem breaks off at a groove.
12. For bends that are not 90 degrees.
13. Bend allowance and setback.
14. Shrinking, stretching, bumping, crimping, and folding.
15. A tolerance indicates a range within which a particular attribute is considered acceptable.
16. Material of the same type and thickness as the original material.
17. The distance from the edge of the sheet to the center of the rivet.
18. To prevent the crack from progressing farther into the material. The hole at the end of the crack removes the sharp stress-concentration area.
19. Total thickness of the metal plus 1-1/2 times the rivet diameter.
20. Plain (1100), cross (5056), tit (2017), dimple (2117), and double dash (2024).

CHAPTER 5
Aircraft Welding

Section A - Fill in the Blanks
1. gas, electric arc, electric resistance
2. 6300, acetylene, oxygen
3. stir welding
4. Metal Inert Gas (MIG) welding
5. DC straight polarity, AC
6. spot, seam
7. argon, argon/helium or argon/nitrogen
8. colorless, odorless, tasteless
9. green, right hand
10. temperature
11. upright, liquid acetone
12. bigger
13. neutral, carburizing, and oxidizing
14. 6300, oxygen
15. backfire, overheating, loose
16. acetylene, oxygen
17. low carbon, low alloy
18. flux
19. silver, oxygen
20. foot pedal, torch mounted
21. longitudinally, radially
22. AC, cleaning action, surface oxides
23. color, silver
24. bead, groove, fillet, and lap joint
25. warping, a buckling
26. inner
27. formed steel patch plate
28. split sleeve
29. nonrepairable, welded
30. larger diameter

Section A - True or False
1. False - Gas, electric arc, and electric resistance welding.
2. False - Most common for material under 3/16
3. True
4. True
5. False - The rod is not consumed during welding
6. True - Plasma arc can cut all electrically conductive metals.
7. False - Never higher than 15 psi.
8. True
9. False - Prevents a high pressure flame or fuel mixture being pushed back into either cylinder causing an explosion.
10. True
11. False - The light intensity of arc welding is much higher and different lenses are required.
12. False - welding tips have one hole; cutting tips several holes
13. False - open acetylene valve before the oxygen valve.
14. True - Neutral flame at 5,850°F; carburizing flame at 5,700
15. False - Always turn off the acetylene valve first
16. True
17. False - Maintain a neutral flame for most steels and a slight excess of acetylene for stainless steel
18. True
19. False - Magnesium is done with a neutral flame.
20. False - Thoriated and zirconiated electrodes have better electron emission characteristics.
21. True
22. False - DC straight polarity
23. True
24. True
25. False - Use welded split sleeve reinforcements.

Section B - Knowledge Application
1. Gas shielded arc welding.
2. If ignited it is extremely hard to extinguish.
3. The weld zone must be shielded with an inert gas.
4. To have the base metal chemically clean without the slightest film of oxide.
5. A neutral flame.
6. Weld a formed steel patch plate over the dented area.
7. Cool the inner sleeve with dry ice or in cold water.
8. By using a larger tip and adjusting the pressures.
9. Gas shielded arc welding.
10. The acetylene, to allow gas in the tip to burn out.
11. Tack welding at intervals along the joint.
12. Turn off the valves and relieve all pressure.
13. They must be re-heat treated.
14. A low strength weld.
15. Metallic arc welding.
16. A gas is used as a shield around the arc to prevent the atmosphere from contaminating the weld.
17. The weld is stronger, more ductile, and more corrosion resistant.
18. Gas, electric arc, and electric resistance.
19. The amount of heat, not the temperature.

ANSWERS

20. Neutral, reducing, and oxidizing flames.
21. Chromium-molybdenum
22. The thickness of the metal.
23. Heat-treatable filler rod.
24. To avoid cracking caused by expansion.
25. At an angle of about 30° from a centerline.
26. It is a tubular joint used in joining two pieces of tubing end to end, in which the edges are cut to resemble a fish's mouth.
27. Because it has a greater length of welded seam.
28. A rosette weld is a round plug weld. Rosette welds are generally used to fuse an inner reinforcing tube (liner) with the outer member.
29. By using fixtures.
30. The tank must be thoroughly purged of any fuel or oil fumes before the welding is begun.

CHAPTER 6
Aircraft Wood and Structural Repair

Section A - Fill in the Blanks
1. 8-12%, 20%
2. decay, musty, moldy
3. temperature, humidity, deterioration
4. shear
5. decay, rot, Decay
6. water penetration
7. compression
8. sharp or solid
9. spruce
10. plywood
11. softwoods
12. grain direction
13. mineral streaks
14. cracks
15. compression
16. casein glue, plastic resin glue, resorcinol glue, epoxy
17. wetting tests
18. full strength, stress
19. scarf joints
20. wing attachment, landing gear, engine mount fittings.

Section A - True or False
1. True - A certificated mechanic may not perform work unless he has performed the work concerned at an earlier date.
2. False - Ideal range is 8-12%.
3. True
4. False - Shear loads
5. True
6. False - The condition of the fabric provides an useful indication of the condition of the wood underneath.
7. True
8. True - Soft and mushy area is an indication of rotting.
9. False - Spruce is the preferred choice.
10. False - softwoods
11. True
12. False - Hard knots are acceptable under certain conditions.
13. False

14. True
15. True
16. False - Surfaces should be prepared with a planer or joiner.
17. True
18. False - Any point except at wing attachment fittings, landing gear, engine mount, or lift and interplace strut fittings.
19. True
20. True

Section B - Knowledge Application
1. Two or more layers glued together with the grain of all layers approximately parallel.
2. It is usually made of an odd number of thin plies with the grain of each layer at 45 or 90 degrees to the adjacent ply or plies. Laminated wood all grain are parallel.
3. Spruce.
4. Inspect for a dark discoloration of the wood surface or gray stains along the grain.
5. Casein (obsolete), plastic resin glue, resorcinol glue, and epoxy resin.
6. Curing time as well as joint strength. Curing time will be shorter and the joint strength will increase.
7. If inspection fails to reveal any decay.
8. Yes, hard knots up to 3/4 inch in diameter are acceptable under certain conditions.
9. It is detrimental to strength and is difficult to recognize, compression wood is characterized by high specific gravity.
10. To determine whether or not they are harmless, or preliminary, or advanced decay.
11. Prevent crushing the wood when the bolts are tightened.
12. Weak and strong areas in the same joint.
13. Clamps, elastic straps, weight, vacuum bags, brads, nails, screws, and electric and hydraulic presses.
14. A scarf joint.
15. The effective glue area will be reduced if both beveled cuts are not the same.
16. The same type of plywood as the original.
17. The use of waxed paper or release films between the patch and pressure plate.
18. Under a wing attachment fitting, landing gear fitting, engine mount fitting, and lift and interplane strut fittings.
19. To provide additional bearing surface.
20. 70°F.

CHAPTER 7
Advanced Composite Materials

Section A - Fill in the Blanks
1. high strength; relatively low weight; corrosion resistance
2. fairings, control surfaces, landing gear doors, leading and trailing edge panels, interior components, floor beams and boards, stabilizer primary structure on new generation large aircraft, turbine engine fan blades, propellers.

ANSWERS

3. fiber and matrix
4. wing spoilers; fairings; ailerons; flaps; nacelles; floor boards; rudders
5. insulating properties; energy absorption and/or redirection; smooth cell walls; moisture and chemical resistance; environmentally compatible; aesthetically pleasing; relatively low cost.
6. high compressive strength; resistance to water penetration.
7. delamination; resin starved areas; resin rich areas; blisters/air bubbles; wrinkles; voids; thermal decomposition
8. improper cure or processing; improper machining; mishandling; improper drilling; tool drops; contamination; improper sanding; substandard material; inadequate tooling; mis-location of holes or details.
9. interlaminar shear ; compression strength
10. scorches, stains, dents, penetration, abrasion, or chips
11. resin starvation, resin richness, wrinkles, ply bridging, discoloration (due to overheating, lightning strike, etc.), impact damage, foreign matter, blisters, disbonding
12. calibration; damage
13. dust; oil; vapors; smoke; moisture
14. secondary bonding
15. nylon; polyester
16. ability to slow or stop fatigue crack growth; replace lost structural area due to corrosion grind-outs; structurally enhance areas with small and negative margins.
17. vertical; controlled; no bleed out; horizontal (or edge)
18. strength requirements
19. potted
20. freeze
21. more
22. lightly loaded; small
23. fiberglass
24. wet lay up, prepreg, DVD, wet lay up
25. special storage, handling, curing
26. honeycomb sandwich, bearing
27. Hi-loks, lockbolts
28. diamond coated, solid carbide, high speed steel
29. flush type
30. higher, lower

Section B - Knowledge Application

1. A homogeneous material has a uniform composition throughout and has no internal physical boundaries.
2. An anisotropic material has mechanical and/or physical properties that vary with direction relative to natural reference axes inherent in the material.
3. Quasi-isotropic material has approximately the same properties as isotropic. An example is a composite laminate with the fibers orientated in the 0°, 90°, +45°, and -45° direction to simulate isotropic properties.
4. More flexibility for layup of complex shapes.
5. Save weight; Minimize resin void size; Maintain fiber orientation during the fabrication process.
6. Nickel-coated graphite cloth; metal meshes; aluminum fiberglass; conductive paints.
7. Low smoke and flammability characteristics.
8. Three – A, B and C stage.
9. In the frozen state the resin of the prepreg material will stay in the B stage of curing. The curing will start when the material is removed from the freezer and heated up again.
10. Panels with complex curves.
11. Small core cells provide better support for sandwich face sheets. Higher density core is stronger and stiffer than lower density core.
12. Too much resin is used. For non-structural applications this is not necessarily bad but it will add weight.
13. Too much resin is bled off during the curing process or if not enough resin is applied during the wet layup process.
14. The method is accomplished by tapping the inspection area with a solid round disk or lightweight hammer-like device and listening to the response of the structure to the hammer.
15. A clear, sharp, ringing sound
16. A dull or thud-like sound
17. Changes within the internal elements of the structure might produce pitch changes that might be interpreted as defects, when in fact they are present by design.
18. Through transmission ultrasonic inspection uses two transducers, one on each side of the area to be inspected. The ultrasonic signal is transmitted from one transducer to the other transducer. The instrument then measures the loss of signal strength. The instrument shows the loss as a percent of the original signal strength or the loss in decibels. The signal loss is compared to a reference standard. Areas with a greater loss than the reference standard indicate a defective area.
19. Cover the unprotected sides of the prepreg material with parting film and clean the area being repaired immediately before laying up the repair plies.
20. Two parts are simultaneously cured. A typical application is the simultaneous cure of a stiffener and a skin.
21. A permanent repair restores the required strength and durability, an interim repair only restores the required strength and has a different inspection interval.
22. A potting repair is heavier than the original control and this could affect the control balance and introduce flutter.
23. Water will boil at cure temperatures and could blow the facesheets of the core.
24. Two holes are drilled on the outside of the delamination area and a low-viscosity resin is injected in one hole till it flows out the other hole.
25. Thick structures or structures made of carbon fiber or Kevlar would block the radar signals.
26. 0°, -45°, 45°, and 90° sequence or in a 0°, -60°, and +60° sequence.
27. Symmetry of lay-up means that for each layer above the midplane of the laminate there must exist an identical layer (same thickness, material properties, and angular orientation) below the midplane. Balance, for every layer centered at some positive angle there must exist an identical layer oriented at a negative angle with the same thickness and material properties.
28. Fiberglass, carbon fiber, and aramid (Kevlar).

ANSWERS

29. Aircraft made from composite materials need additional protection because, for instance, carbon fibers are 1000 times more resistive than aluminum to current flow, and epoxy resin is 1 million times more resistive. Failure to protect composite structures would result in damage because the lighting strike energy cannot be dissipated.
30. Thermoplastic materials are non-curing systems that can be reshaped or reformed after the part has been processed or consolidated. They differ from thermoset materials because they don't chemically cure and can be reshaped.

CHAPTER 8
Aircraft Painting and Finishing

Section A - Fill in the Blanks
1. weight, integrity
2. Polyurethane
3. Dipping, brushing, and spraying
4. spray gun with integral paint container, spray gun with pressure pot
5. siphon feed gun, gravity feed gun, HVLP gun
6. internal, air, fluid
7. preparation
8. upper
9. Crosscoat
10. 50%
11. thinner, reducer
12. loose nozzle, clogged, packing
13. milky haze
14. trapped solvents, air, moisture
15. too much, too close, too slowly
16. bumpy
17. small holes
18. trapped solvents, unequal drying
19. too far, air pressure
20. 3 times

Section A - True or False
1. True
2. True
3. False - Bright yellow.
4. False - If the paint materials are too thin
5. True - 65% or more paint is transferred with HVLP spray gun.
6. False - A HVLP spray gun is an internal mix gun.
7. True
8. True
9. False - Alodine is used to etch the aluminum material.
10. True
11. False - If the spray pattern is offset to one side, the air port in the air cap or the ports in the horn may be plugged.
12. True
13. False - First spray the corners and gaps.
14. True
15. True
16. False - Ensure the surface is clean.
17. False - "N"
18. False - 12" high.
19. False - It is old nitrocellulose finish.
20. True

Section B - Knowledge Application
1. Primers, enamels, urethanes (polyurethane), and epoxies.
2. Environmental concerns; more effective primer formulas.
3. The spray pattern is offset to one side.
4. Bond to the surface, inhibit corrosion, and provide an anchor point for the finish coat.
5. The use of respiratory protection such as fresh air supply or respirator. The use of protective clothing and gloves.
6. Dipping, brushing, and spraying.
7. Incorrect air pressure or the distance of the gun from the work is too large.
8. Too much paint being applied or gun too close to surface.
9. Incorrect paint viscosity, air pressure, gun setting, or distance of the gun from the work.
10. Clouding or blooming of the film.
11. Moisture in the air supply, adverse humidity, or changes in temperature.
12. Orange peel or pin holes due to too fast drying of paint.
13. Synthetic rubber products, composites, fabric, acrylics, and bonded surfaces.
14. It helps to eliminate general corrosion problems.
15. Polyurethane finishing system
16. Use a paint stripper, Plastic blast medium, or mechanical sanding (composite aircraft)
17. Open air valve all the way, set fluid valve to dial 4. Practice on a piece of masking paper and check if the fan shape and amount of paint applied are correct. Close the air valve if a smaller fan shape is required and open the fluid valve if more paint is required. Adjust both valves till the correct settings are achieved before starting the painting process.
18. A loose nozzle, clogged vent hole on the supply cup, or the packing may be leaking around the needle.
19. To ensure that the surface is clean and free from any type of contamination.
20. On the vertical tail surface or on the side of the fuselage.

CHAPTER 9
Aircraft Electrical System

Section A - Fill in the Blanks
1. mathematical, electricity
2. semiconductors, transistors
3. generators, alternators
4. conductor movement/force, magnetic field current
5. inverter, Hz (cycle) AC
6. Inductive, capacitance, phase
7. Inversely, reduced, half
8. impedance, resistance
9. lead-acid, ni-cad, plates
10. essential, thirty
11. potassium hydroxide, discharge, manufacturer's instructions
12. increases, greater, greater

ANSWERS

13. generator control units (GCU), output
14. armature, field, electromagnetic, bus, loads
15. voltage/current, field
16. solid state, AC power, bus
17. alternator housing, integrated drive generator
18. bus power control unit, generator control unit
19. throttle, activated
20. flexing, stranded
21. mega-ohmmeter, condition
22. derating, %
23. voltage drop, satisfactory
24. one, staggered
25. switches, close

Section A - Matching

1-1. C   1-4. D
1-2. D   1-5. A
1-3. B   1-6. B

2-1. A   2-4. C
2-2. B   2-5. A
2-3. B   2-6. C

3-1. C   3-5. A   3-9. B
3-2. D   3-6. D   3-10. D
3-3. C   3-7. C
3-4. B   3-8. A

4-1. C   4-4. D   4-7. C
4-2. A   4-5. B
4-3. B   4-6. A

5-1. E   5-4. F
5-2. C   5-5. D
5-3. A   5-6. B

6-1. F   6-4. D
6-2. C   6-5. B
6-3. A   6-6. E

Section B - Knowledge Application

1. 2.4A
2. 4 ohms
3. 24V
4. 24 × .707 = 17V
5. 112 × 1.41 = 158V
6. $X_L = 2\pi(60)(.175)$ $X_L = 66\Omega$
7. $R_T = \dfrac{1}{\dfrac{1}{10} + \dfrac{1}{15}}$ $R_T = 6\Omega$
8. $Z = \sqrt{R^2 + X_L^2}$ $Z = \sqrt{8^2 + 8^2}$ $Z = 11.3\Omega$
   (Use $X_L = 2\pi fL$ to find X_L in ohms)
   (use $R = E/I$ to find R in ohms)
9. $Z = \sqrt{R^2 + X_C^2}$ $Z = \sqrt{8^2 + 26.5^2}$ $Z = 28\Omega$
   (Use $X_C = 1/(2\pi fC)$ to find X_C in ohms)
10. T.P. = $I^2 \times R$
11. Watts
12. $X_L = 2\pi(400)(.01)$ $X_L = 25\Omega$, $X_C = \dfrac{1}{2\pi \times 400 \times .00015}$
    $X_C = 2.65\Omega$, $Z = \sqrt{\left(\dfrac{1}{40}\right)^2 + \left(\dfrac{1}{25} - \dfrac{1}{2.65}\right)^2}$ $Z = 3\Omega$
13. A.P. = E × 1
14. Volt amps (VA)
15. T.P.= 5^2 × 5.6 T.P.= 140 Watts, A.P. = 50 × 5
    A.P.= 250VA, PF = (140/250) × 100 PF = 56%
16. In between 14 and 12, choose bigger size of 12.
17. Size 20 wire.
18. Size 18 wire (in between 20 and 18).
19. 26.5A
20. 17.2A
21. Automatic reset-type circuit breakers.
22. When used with high rush-in circuits, inductive circuits, and direct current motors.
23. Allowable power loss, permissible voltage drop, and current carrying ability.
24. When starting.
25. As short as practicable.
26. When an overload or circuit fault exists.
27. Four.
28. By the identification code on the wire.
29. A Generator Control Unit (GCU).
30. Twenty-five percent larger than the maximum diameter of the wire bundle.

CHAPTER 10
Aircraft Instrument Systems

Section A - Fill in the Blanks

1. senses; display
2. air; gyroscopes
3. bourbon tube, diaphragm or bellows, solid-state
4. sensed air pressure, digital values
5. pitot static, aircraft systems
6. altitude, pressure, pressure
7. true airspeed
8. machmeter
9. synchro
10. electro, permanent
11. crankshaft
12. tachometer probes, tach generator
13. forces, inertial reference
14. ADC
15. direction, angle
16. vacuum systems, pressure systems, electrical systems
17. artificial horizon, pitch, roll.
18. laterally, vertically, longitudinally
19. sensing elements, computing elements, output elements, command elements
20. attitude, electric attitude indicators
21. ECAM
22. flight management system (FMS)
23. flight, engine, airframe
24. 24
25. electromagnetic, electrical

ANSWERS

Section A - True or False
1. True
2. False - Flight, engine, navigation.
3. True
4. False - An aneroid.
5. False - Remote
6. True
7. True
8. True
9. False - Direct current systems often use DC Selsyn systems.
10. True
11. True
12. False - Pushes the control yoke forwards to lower the nose.
13. True
14. False - Total air temperature is the static air temperature plus any rise in temperature caused by high speed movement of the aircraft through the air.
15. True
16. False - Swinging the compass is the process for adjusting magnetic deviation.
17. True
18. False - The magnetic compass is not a sensing element of the autopilot system.
19. True
20. False - Attitude indicator and directional gyro.
21. True
22. True
23. False - The master caution light can be canceled.
24. False - Low frequency.
25. True

Section B - Knowledge Application
1. Aircraft Specification; Type Certificate Data Sheets; Flight Manuals.
2. Caution.
3. A sensitive altimeter.
4. Scale, hysteresis, and installation.
5. Rate of climb, Airspeed, and Altimeter.
6. A leak test.
7. Vacuum, air pressure, or electricity.
8. Transmits information from one point to another point.
9. Crankshaft or Main Turbine Rotor Speed.
10. A thermocouple-type system.
11. Correct for deviations by adjusting compensating magnets.
12. Flight Instruments, Engine Instruments, Navigation Instruments.
13. The total exhaust pressure to the pressure of the ram air at the inlet of the engine.
14. Air Data Computer (ADC).
15. Vane type which uses an alpha vane externally mounted to the outside of the fuselage; probe type which uses two slots in a probe that extends out of the side of the fuselage.
16. Cylinder head temperature in reciprocating engines and exhaust gas temperature in turbine engines.
17. EICAS
18. EICAS
19. Certificated A&P mechanics can remove, inspect, troubleshoot, and perform operation checks of instruments.
20. EICAS or ECAM, Air DATA Computer, thrust management computer, EIFIS symbol generators, ADFS, Inertial reference system, collision avoidance system, radio navigational aids.

CHAPTER 11
Communication and Navigation

Section A - Fill in the Blanks
1. valence shells
2. holes, eight
3. shockley, three-layer
4. power, inverter
5. polarity, channel
6. open, closed
7. LEDs, color
8. ratio, base
9. base, larger
10. NAND
11. upper, horizontal situation
12. 90°, 90°
13. carrier, frequency
14. superior, radio
15. detector/demodulator
16. polarized, direction
17. conductive, antenna(s)
18. frequency, Morse code
19. NDB, null
20. RMI
21. glideslope, 3°
22. radar beacon, location
23. avoidance, transponder
24. radome
25. three, latitude/longitude

Section A - True or False
1. False - Certified Repair Station
2. False - Continuous
3. True
4. True
5. True
6. False - Conductor
7. True
8. False - Directly proportional.
9. True
10. False - Base
11. False - Less
12. True
13. False - High current gains.
14. False - Magnetic
15. True
16. True
17. False
18. False - Inversely proportional.
19. True
20. False - 136.975 MHz
21. True
22. False - Stable oscillating frequency.

ANSWERS

23. True
24. False - 90° to the length of the antenna.
25. False - 2°
26. False - Inactive
27. True
28. False - 7500
29. False - AGL
30. True

Section B - Knowledge Application
1. Changing signal's amplitude, frequency, or phase.
2. Size and inability to withstand vibration made them susceptible to damage.
3. Combines readily with itself and form a lattice of atoms in which adjacent atoms share electrons to fill out the valence shell. Can be easily doped to create N-type and P-type semiconductor material.
4. The negative battery terminal is attached to the p-material and attracts holes away from the junction in the diode. Positive terminal attached to the N- material attracting the free electrons from in the opposite direction. Current cannot flow through the circuit when this occurs.
5. When reversed biased, only leakage current flows through the diode unless it is equipped with a zener voltage. When the zener voltage is reached the diode lets current flow freely through the diode in the direction it is normally blocked. Zener diodes can be used to as a means of dropping voltage or voltage regulation as well as step down circuit voltage for a particular application.
6. Stable in a wide range of temperatures; reduce the overall number of components used saving money and increasing reliability.
7. Switching devices and SCR (with slight modification)
8. Common-emitter amplifier; common-collector amplifier; common-base amplifier.
9. If the input to the gate is Logic 1 then the output is NOT logic 1. A NOT gate inverts the input signal. If there is voltage at the input, there would be no output voltage.
10. In an OR gate if any one of the Logic inputs is a 1 then the output will be a 1. In EXCLUSIVE if both logic inputs are 1 then the output is 0 instead of 1.
11. An AC generator is placed at the midpoint of an antenna. As current builds and collapses in the antenna, a magnetic field does so around it. An electric field also builds and subsides as the voltage shifts from one end of the antenna to the other. Both fields fluctuate around the antenna at the same time. At any point along the antenna, voltage and current vary inversely to each other. Each new current flow creates new fields around the antenna that forces the not totally collapsed fields from the aircraft out into space.
12. Process of removing the original information signal from the carrier wave.
13. FM has a steady current flow and requires less power to produce, since modulating an oscillator takes less power than modulating the amplitude.
14. Original carrier wave, carrier wave plus the modulating frequency, carrier wave minus modulating frequency

15. A receiver is needed to isolate the desired carrier wave with its information. It separates data signal from the carrier wave. It amplifies the desired frequency captured by the antenna which is weak from traveling through atmosphere.
16. Length, polarization, and directivity.
17. A metal fuselage creates a ground plane that acts as the missing one-quarter length.
18. The orientation of electric and electromagnetic fields remain at 90°, but radiate from the antenna with varying strength in different directions. The strength of the radiated field varies depending on the type of antenna and the angular proximity to it. All antennas radiate a stronger signal in some directions compared to others.
19. A dipole antenna is a conductor and sometimes known as the Hertz antenna. AC transmission current is fed to a dipole antenna. Current is strongest in the middle of the antenna about half the wavelength of the transmission frequency in length. It is horizontally polarized. Common as VOR antenna. Marconi antennas are 1/4 wave for VHF communication. They are vertically polarized and create omni-directional field. Loop antennas are, as their name implies, fashioned into a loop which alters its field characteristics significantly. It is more compact and less prone to damage. It is used as a receiving antenna and is highly direction-sensitive.
20. Bearing degrees to or from the station.
21. Localizer-provides horizontal guidance to the centerline of the runway; glideslope-provides vertical guidance to the touchdown point; compass locator aids in intercepting the approach navigation aid system; marker beacon provides distance from the runway.
22. It transmits in such a way that the aircraft's target symbol is highlighted on the PPI to be distinguishable.
23. Required internationally in aircraft with more than 30 seats or more than 15,000 kg. It provides advisories similar to TCAS I but also analyzes the flightpath of approaching aircraft.
24. Entire airspace covered at lower expense. Provides more accurate data as vector state is generated from the aircraft. Weather is a reduced factor. Ultra-high frequency GPS is not affected. Increased accuracy allows higher density traffic flow. The higher degree of control enables routing for fewer weather delays and optimum fuel burn rates.
25. Space segment, control segment, and user segment.
26. Very high frequency (VHF) system.
27. Every 24 calendar months.
28. One for the localizer, and one for the glide slope receivers.
29. Vertical guidance for correct angle of descent.
30. A VHF communications receiver tuned to 121.5 MHz.

CHAPTER 12
Hydraulic and Pneumatic Power Systems

Section A - Fill in the Blanks
1. 100, negligible
2. mineral, polyalphaolefin, phosphate ester
3. Skydrol, IV, V

ANSWERS

4. seals, gaskets, hoses
5. micron, particle
6. cold start, pump ripples, shock loads
7. engine gearbox, electric motor
8. non-pressurized, bleed air
9. screening straining, preventing
10. cleaning, replacing
11. differential, operating principle, loaded
12. manually reset, permanent
13. power-driven, hand, engine driven
14. positive, non-positive
15. shear, in the middle of, smaller
16. electrically, servo, servo
17. diverts, pressure
18. priority, non-critical, low
19. burst, preserves
20. failure, rupture, excessive
21. thermal, thermal expansion
22. regulators, pump
23. shuttle, seal off
24. system, components
25. preload

Section A - True or False
1. False - 3,000-5,000
2. True
3. False - All contaminants are bad.
4. False - Filters cleaned or replaced.
5. False - All of the following.
6. True
7. False - Non-pressurized.
8. False - 5 microns.
9. True
10. False - Compensator controlled.
11. True
12. True
13. True
14. True
15. True

Section B - Knowledge Application
1. Red.
2. Material will be damaged, softened and/or peeled.
3. A shear section in the pump-drive shaft.
4. All lines should be plugged or capped after disconnecting.
5. A clogged filter.
6. Hand pumps, engine-driven pumps, electrically driven pumps, and air driven (bleed air).
7. Cabin pressurization, bleed air, aspirator and venture-tee, and hydraulic system pressure.
8. Limit amount of pressure preventing failure of components.
9. To manage the output of the pump to maintain system pressure and allow the pump to turn without resistance.
10. An accumulator
11. To control the rate of airflow
12. To remove contamination and moisture
13. Make sure the air or preload has been discharged.
14. No; petroleum base and phosphate ester fluids will not mix. Neither are seals for one fluid usable with others.
15. In a closed center system the fluid is always pressurized when the pump runs and therefore it will be faster then the open center system that needs to be built up pressure. Since most aircraft applications require instantaneous operation, closed center systems are the most widely used.
16. The advantage of the powerpack is that there is no need for a centralized hydraulic power supply system and long stretches of hydraulic lines which reduces weight.
17. Required because the reservoirs are often located in wheel wells or other non-pressurized areas of the aircraft and at high altitude there is not enough atmospheric pressure to move the fluid to the pump inlet.
18. Bypass relief valve opens if the filter clogs this will permit continued hydraulic flow and operation of aircraft systems.
19. Centrifugal and impeller pumps.
20. The angle of the pump starts to decrease when the system pressure reaches about 2,850 psi. The output of the pump will decrease to adjust to system demand.
21. System pressure will increase.
22. Some controlled by pressure, some mechanically, some by electric switches.
23. The PTU is able to transfer power but not fluid between two hydraulic systems. For instance if the engine driven pump in the #1 system is inoperative than system pressure in the number 2 can power the PTU to power the number 1 system.
24. EDV solenoid will move up creating a path for the outlet pressure (P_S) to reach the top of the compensator valve. The outlet pressure will push the compensator valve down and the output pressure will act on the yoke actuating piston and reduce the yoke angle and pump output is reduced to zero.
25. Pressure-reducing valves are used in hydraulic systems where it is necessary to lower the normal system operating pressure a specified amount.
26. (A). Dampen pressure surges in the hydraulic system caused by actuation of a unit and the effort of the pump to maintain pressure at a preset level. (B). Aid or supplement the power pump when several units are operating at once by supplying extra power from its "accumulated" or stored power. (C). Store power for the limited operation of a hydraulic unit when the pump is not operating. (D). Supply fluid under pressure to compensate for small internal or external (not desired) leaks which would cause the system to cycle continuously by action of the pressure switches continually "kicking in."
27. To provide electrical and hydraulic power if the aircraft loses electrical or hydraulic power.
28. When pressurized nitrogen is not directly used to actuate the landing gear actuators or brake units, it will apply the pressurized nitrogen to move hydraulic fluid to the actuator.
29. The engine driven pump won't be able to draw fluid from the tank, and only the AC driven pump can supply fluid to essential systems.

ANSWERS

CHAPTER 13
Aircraft Landing Gear Systems

Section A - Fill in the Blanks
1. tail wheel, tandem, tricycle landing gear
2. fairings, wheel pants.
3. spring steel, aluminum, composite materials.
4. torque links, torque arms
5. locating cam assembly (centering cam)
6. camber
7. powerpack
8. emergency extension system
9. landing gear retraction test, swinging
10. shimmy damper
11. thermal plugs
12. torqued
13. lack of lubrication, bluish
14. excessive impact, indentations
15. top, right
16. transfer plate, rotors, stators
17. carbon disc brake
18. independent system, booster system, power brake system
19. hydraulic system
20. take off
21. skid, imminent
22. skidding
23. gravity, pressure
24. skidding
25. chevron

Section A - True or False
1. False - Most use a nosewheel steering system.
2. True
3. False - Filled with nitrogen and hydraulic fluid.
4. False - Nitrogen in the tires and the shock strut combine to smooth out bumps.
5. True
6. True
7. False - Hydraulic pressure.
8. True
9. False - On high performance; not small single engine aircraft.
10. False - Being down and locked.
11. True
12. False - Modern aircraft use two piece wheels
13. False - Inner halves have provisions for brake rotors.
14. True - If the wheel bolts have failed the axle nut could be the only thing that keeps the wheel halves together.
15. True
16. False - Segmented rotor disc brakes are used on large transport category aircraft
17. True
18. True
19. False - The anti skid system provides input to the auto-brake system to prevent brake skid.
20. True
21. False - Type VII tires are high performance for jet aircraft.
22. True
23. False - 3 hours.
24. False - Deflate the tire before removing or probing any area where a foreign object is lodged.
25. True

Section B - Knowledge Application
1. Dry air or nitrogen, and hydraulic fluid.
2. Clean and inspect for damage and proper extension.
3. They keep the main landing gear wheels pointed in a straight ahead direction.
4. Hydraulic, or electrical.
5. A simple system consisting of mechanical linkage hooked to the rudder pedals.
6. A shimmy damper or in large aircraft using power steering the power steering actuators provide the dampening.
7. They reduce the pressure to the brakes and increase the volume of fluid flow.
8. Independent, power boost, and power control.
9. Pressurize the system.
10. A rubber O-ring between the two wheel halves.
11. Proper tire inflation.
12. Rapid or uneven wear near the edge of tread, and creep or slip when the brakes are applied.
13. During an annual or other inspections, when landing gear components have been replaced, and after hard landings.
14. Discoloration (blue color).
15. To bring a fast moving aircraft to a stop during ground roll without tire skidding.
16. To relieve air pressure when the tire overheats due to hard braking or extended taxiing to prevent tire blowout.
17. Gravity and pressure methods.
18. Mechanical (cables, linkages), electrical, or hydraulic.
19. Nosewheel centering internal cams or external track.
20. Carbon brakes
21. Tricycle or conventional.
22. They consist of single, tapered strips or tubes of strong spring steel material. One end of the strut is bolted to the heavy structure of the aircraft under the cabin area, and the axles are bolted to the opposite ends.
23. The spring oleo strut is using a spring as preload and the air-oleo strut uses nitrogen as a preload.
24. The metering pin restricts the flow of fluid from the lower part of the cylinder to the upper part when the cylinder is being compressed during landing or taxiing.
25. Centering cams or springs to align the wheels straight ahead.
26. The truck is located on the bottom of the strut piston and has the axles attached to it. A truck is used when wheels are to be placed in tandem (one behind the other) or in a dual-tandem arrangement.
27. Nitrogen or Air bottle, Mechanical hand crank or ratchet, emergency hydraulic system using handpump, and mechanical system so that the uplocks can be unlocked and the gear can free fall to the down and locked position.
28. Skid gear.
29. The brand name or name of the manufacturer responsible for compliance, and the country of

ANSWERS

manufacture if manufactured outside the United States; the size, ply rating, and serial number; the qualification test speed and skid depth when the test speed is greater than 160mph and the word "reinforced" if applicable; and the applicable TSO number.
30. It is easier to change tires.

CHAPTER 14
Aircraft Fuel System

Section A - Fill in the Blanks
1. hard engine starting, slow warm-up, slow
2. explode, detonate
3. vaporizes, carburetor
4. 30-40°F, humid
5. explosion, pressure, temperature
6. lower, higher
7. main, auxiliary, surge
8. rigid removable tanks, bladder tanks, integral fuel
9. sump
10. wiring
11. gate, plug
12. quickly
13. engine driven fuel pump
14. positive, vapor lock
15. vane type
16. crossfeed system, fuel transfer
17. large, fuel system
18. micronic, 10-25
19. fuel heaters
20. Direct Current (DC)
21. Stain, seep, heavy seep, running
22. 1-1/2 inches, 4 inches
23. dried and ventilated, combustible gas indicator
24. cloudy
25. Over the wing, pressure refueling

Section A - True or False
1. True
2. False - Turbine fuel has a higher flash point than AVGAS
3. True
4. False - Higher cylinder head temperature.
5. True
6. False - Jet-A is the most common.
7. False - Pump feed system.
8. True
9. True
10. False - Aircraft equipped with integral fuel tanks have fuel vent systems and fuel jettison systems dump fuel when the take off weight is higher than the landing weight.
11. True
12. False - To the engine driven fuel pump.
13. False - Variable displacement pump.
14. False - Lowest part of the tank.
15. True
16. True
17. False - Electronic fuel quantity systems have no moving part which is one of their advantages.
18. True
19. False - They measure fuel mass.
20. True
21. False - Must be repaired before the next flight because vapors in these areas could cause a fire or explosion.
22. True
23. False - Organisms do not grow in AVGAS, only turbine fuel.
24. True
25. True

Section B - Knowledge Application
1. If take off weight is higher than the landing weight, in an emergency these aircraft need to reduce the weight to a specified landing weight.
2. Rigid removable cell, bladder-type cell, integral fuel cell.
3. The structure of the cavity that the cell fits into.
4. Alerts the flight crew that there may be danger of ice crystals forming in the fuel.
5. To provide an interconnected fuel system so that fuel can be fed from various tanks to any engine.
6. Crossfeed, transfer, ON or OFF.
7. Compare the fuel quantity in the tank with the indication of the electronic fuel quantity system.
8. An underwing or single-point pressure fueling system.
9. Reduces fueling time, eliminates aircraft skin damage, and reduces chances of contamination.
10. The tank is pressurized with up to 1/2 psi air pressure and liquid soap is added to detect leaks.
11. An internal component fuel leak (shutoff valve, selector valve, or crossfeed valve).
12. Sight glass, mechanical, electrical, and electronic.
13. It measures by weight instead of volume.
14. Resist surging from changes in the attitude of the aircraft.
15. Allow water and sediment to settle to the drain point.
16. Drain the water out of the tanks.
17. The structure of the inside of the wing is used as a fuel tank and sealant is used at joints and rivet holes to seal the structure so that it won't leak.
18. The bladder is held in place by several "buttons" or "snaps," which attach the bladder to the top, bottom, and sides of the compartment.
19. The word FUEL and the proper type and the minimum grade of fuel approved for use in the aircraft.
20. The ejector pump works on the Venturi principle.
21. The rotor holds the sliding vanes and is installed in the liner with its axis of rotation eccentric to the axis of the liner. When the rotor is turning, the vanes maintain a constant contact with the surface of the liner. Fuel enters the inlet port and is forced by sliding vanes through the outlet port. The floating pin aligns the sliding vanes against the surface of the liner.
22. Mounted with the electric motor on the outside of the fuel tank or the entire pump and motor are located inside the fuel tank.
23. Fuel temperature or a differential pressure type indicators.

ANSWERS

24. The warning switch is operated by the pressure differential developed as pressure on the input side of the filter increases owing to filter clogging.
25. To prevent ice crystals in the fuel from clogging system filters.
26. Fuel vent systems are designed to prevent the buildup of pressure in the fuel tanks and allow proper flow of fuel from the tanks. The fuel vent system maintains the fuel tanks at near-ambient atmospheric pressure under all operating conditions.
27. It is required when the maximum takeoff weight exceeds the maximum landing weight.
28. A light that indicates when the valve is in motion.
29. Any fuel tank may supply fuel to any engine.
30. They should be removed and replaced with new ones.

CHAPTER 15
Ice and Rain Protection

Section A - Fill in the Blanks
1. airfoils and air inlets
2. moisture, freezing temperatures
3. lighter, of little
4. rime, clear
5. icing, performance, deteriorate
6. thermal, electrical, and chemical anti-icing systems
7. turbine compressor, engine exhaust heat exchangers, combustion heater.
8. computers
9. electric thermal
10. weeping wing
11. pneumatic deicing system, leading edge
12. vacuum, suction
13. engine-driven air pump (vacuum pump), gas turbine compressors
14. electrical boots or chemical deice
15. ice, fog
16. resistance wire, conductive coating
17. ice detector sensors

Section A - True or False
1. True
2. True
3. True
4. True
5. True
6. False
7. False
8. True
9. False
10. True
11. False
12. True
13. False
14. True
15. True

Section B - Knowledge Application
1. Clear and rime ice.
2. A). Malformation of the airfoil which could decrease the amount of lift. B). Additional weight and unequal formation of the ice which could cause unbalancing of the aircraft.
3. Surge, vibration, and complete thrust loss.
4. Wing leading edges; horizontal and vertical stabilizer leading edges; engine cowl leading edges; propellers, propeller spinner; air data probes; flight deck windows; water and waste system lines and drains.
5. Heat surfaces with hot air; heat with electrical elements; breaking up ice with inflatable boots; chemical spray.
6. Wing, leading edge slats, horizontal and vertical stabilizer, engine, and wind shield anti-ice.
7. To heat both wings equally, keeping the airplane aerodynamically stable in icing conditions.
8. Without a forward speed the leading edge can easily overheat if left on, therefore the ground sensing system (weight on wheels) will disable the system.
9. Antifreeze solution is pumped from a reservoir through a mesh screen embedded in the leading edges of the wings and stabilizers. Activated by a switch in the cockpit, the liquid flows over the wing and tail surfaces, deicing as it flows.
10. When deice system is energized, the control valves in each nacelle and deflate valve receive power. The deice control valves route pressurized air from the discharge side of the pump to the deicer boots. At 17 psi, pressure switches on the deflate valve will de-energize the deice control valves, and the boots will be deflated and vacuum pressure will hold the boots down against the leading edge surfaces.
11. A new layer of ice may begin to form on the expanded boots and become unremovable.
12. Large amounts of hot air can be bled off the compressor, providing a satisfactory source of anti-icing and deicing heat.
13. Pumps have carbon vanes and parts that self lubricate.
14. Windshield wipers, chemical rain repellent, pneumatic rain removal (jet blast), or the windshields are treated with a hydrophobic surface seal coating.
15. An engine-driven air pump and bleed air from a turbine-engine compressor.
16. In a wet-type air pump, it is used to remove entrained oil from output air before it is sent through the boot system.
17. To prevent the buildup of static charges on the boots.
18. Suction is supplied to the boots during flight.
19. Combustion heaters or engine bleed air.
20. By mixing heated air with ambient (cold) air.
21. The airflow is exhausted to the atmosphere.
22. Wipers, pneumatic (jet blast), chemical rain repellent, and windshields treated with a hydrophobic surface seal coating.
23. Electrical or hydraulic power.
24. Aerodynamic forces reduce blade pressure; Failure to achieve fast enough wiper oscillations.
25. The air blast breaks the rains drops into small particles that are then blown away.

CHAPTER 16
Cabin Environmental Control Systems

Section A - Fill in the Blanks
1. Colorless, odorless, tasteless
2. Aviator Breathing Oxygen
3. 50, water vapor
4. Demand-flow
5. Diluter-demand, pressure-demand
6. Moisture
7. 8,000 ft, cruising altitude
8. Pressurization, depressurization
9. Supercharger, turbocharger, engine driven compressor

ANSWERS

10. Bleed air
11. Isobaric, differential
12. Cabin altitude, rate of change, barometric pressure
13. Outflow valve
14. Electrically, cabin pressure controller
15. Over pressurization
16. Negative relief valves
17. Vapor cycle, air cycle
18. Engine compressor, APU
19. Refrigeration turbine unit, air cycle machine
20. Thermistors, resistance
21. Liquid, vapor
22. Receiver dryer
23. Copper, aluminum
24. Exhaust gases
25. Cleaning filters, spark plug

Section A - True or False
1. True
2. False - they are painted green.
3. True
4. False - Indicates that the pressure relief valve has opened and this should be investigated.
5. True
6. True
7. False - Below 8,000.
8. True
9. False - Turbochargers are the most common.
10. False - Turbochargers are driven by exhaust gases.
11. True
12. False - Differential control mode of a cabin pressurization system controls pressure to maintain a constant pressure between the air outside the cabin and the ambient air.
13. True
14. False - Prevent cabin over pressurization.
15. True
16. True
17. False - A swirling motion will separate the water droplets.
18. True
19. False - It is an closed system.
20. False - R134-A has replaced R12.
21. True
22. False - Should feel cool.
23. True
24. False - Use a exhaust shroud heating system.
25. False - Drawn from an aircraft fuel tank.

Section B - Knowledge Application
1. Outflow valve.
2. Bleed air from the turbine engine compressor.
3. The cabin pressure controller.
4. Gasoline combustion heater, electric heater, and exhaust shroud heat exchanger.
5. Carry the heat where it is needed.
6. Expansion turbine, air-to-air heat exchangers, water separator, and various temperature control valves.
7. The compressed air turns a turbine, and it undergoes a pressure and temperature drop.
8. Moist air passes through a fiberglass bag that condenses the moisture in droplets, vanes swirl the air and droplets are collected and drained.
9. The compressor pressurizes low pressure vapor into high pressure vapor. The condenser cools the high pressure vapor with outside air and turns it into a high pressure liquid. At the expansion valve the high pressure liquid changes into a low pressure liquid. In evaporator the low pressure liquid absorbs cabin heat and change into a low pressure vapor and returns to the receiver dryer where the process is repeated again.
10. When the pack valve opens hot high pressure bleed air flows to air mix valve. Depending on temperature a certain amount of this bleed air travels to the mixing chamber and the rest flows to the primary heat exchanger to be cooled. The bleed air will travel through a second mixing valve and enters the compressor of the air cycle machine. The pressure and temperature of the bleed air increases. The bleed air will flow through the secondary heat exchanger where its temperature is lowered by ambient air. After the secondary heat exchanger the air enters the air cycle machine. Here the air temperature lowers because energy in the air drives the turbine which in turn drives the compressor. The shape of the turbine blades expand the air which lowers in pressure and temperature. The air that leaves the air cycle machine flows through the water separator where moisture is removed. When the sensor at the water separator senses 35 degrees the anti-ice control valve opens to allow warmer air to mix with the air leaving the air cycle machine. The air that leaves the water separator will flow to the mixing chamber where it is mixed with hot bleed air. Temperature control is realized by positioning the two mixing valves so that the desired temperature is achieved.
11. A receiver dryer, evaporator, compressor, condenser, and expansion valve.
12. Oxygen flows from a charged cylinder through a high pressure line to a reducing valve and to mask outlets.
13. System must be purged to remove moisture.
14. Dry nitrogen, dry air, or oxygen.
15. Aviators' breathing oxygen.
16. Provide lubrication and prevent compressor failure.
17. Use oil free tools, clothing, hands, adequate eye protection.
18. Turbocharger, supercharger, engine driven compressor.
19. Small amount of LOX can be converted to an enormous amount of gaseous oxygen, thus needing little storage space.
20. Cabin altitude, rate of change, and barometric correction and pressurization mode.
21. Cracks in the exhaust system could allow exhaust fumes to enter the cabin of the airplane, which could cause carbon dioxide poisoning.
22. The same fuel that is used for the aircraft.
23. Because the moisture can freeze at the expansion valve and stopping the flow of refrigerant in the system.
24. The purpose of aircraft cabin pressurization is to maintain a comfortable environment for aircraft

ANSWERS

occupants while allowing the aircraft to operate efficiently at high altitudes.
25. Supercharger, turbocharger, cabin pressure compressors, bleed air, or electrical cabin compressors.
26. Bleed air from the turbine-engine compressor.
27. The maximum cabin differential depends on the structural strength of the aircraft structure. If the pressure gets too high the structure will fail.
28. The outflow valve.
29. To prevent that the pressure inside the aircraft becomes lower than the outside pressure. The structure is not designed to withstand a negative pressure.
30. Set the rate of cabin altitude change, cabin pressure altitude, and barometric correction.

CHAPTER 17
Fire Protection Systems

Section A - Fill in the Blanks
1. a fixed fire protection
2. thermal switch system, thermocouple system, continuous loop detector system.
3. rate of temperature rise, slowly
4. chromel and constantan
5. thermistor, Lingberg
6. nacelle temperature
7. AND
8. Systron-Donner, Meggitt safety systems
9. lavatories, cargo, smoke
10. flame detectors
11. reciprocating, carbon monoxide, exhaust system
12. water, ignition
13. Carbon dioxide
14. high Rate of Discharge (HRD), 1 to 2
15. liquid, gas

Section A - True or False
1. True   4. False   7. True   10. True
2. False   5. True   8. True
3. False   6. False   9. False

Section B - Knowledge Application
1. Engines and APU, Cargo and baggage compartments, Lavatories, Electronic bays, Wheel wells, Bleed air ducts.
2. Overheat detectors, Rate-of-temperature-rise detectors, Flame detectors, Observation by crew members.
3. Rate-of-temperature-rise detectors, Radiation sensing detectors, Smoke detectors, Overheat detectors, CO_2 detectors, Combustible mixture detectors, Optical detectors.
4. Fenwal, Kidde, and Lingberg
5. Precise fit, eliminates chafing, and quick and easy to install.
6. Fire detection and extinguishing for engines, APUs, cargo bays, and bleed air systems.
7. Halocarbon Clean Agents, Halon, and dry powders.
8. Turbine engines, APU, Cargo compartments, and lavatories.
9. Cartridge (squib) and frangible disc type valve.
10. To rupture the frangible disk.
11. This is an indication for the maintenance crew that the fire extinguishing system was activated by the flight crew.
12. The engine will stop because the fuel control shuts off, the engine will be isolated from the aircraft systems, and the fire extinguishing system will be activated.
13. The presence of a fire would be easily discovered by a crew member while at his station; and each part of the compartment is easily accessible in flight.
14. Class B has a smoke detector or fire detection system.
15. The master warning lights come on, the fire warning aural operates, a cargo fire warning message shows, the cargo fire warning light comes on.
16. Kinks and sharp bends can cause an internal wire to short intermittently to the outer tubing and cause false alarms.
17. 550 psi.
18. The thermal switch, called a spot detector, works by the expansion of the outer case of the unit. When the detector is exposed to heat, the case becomes longer and causes the two contacts inside the case to be drawn together. When the contacts meet, the electrical circuit is completed and the alarm activates.

The thermocouple is made of two dissimilar metals, such as Chromel and constantan, which are twisted together and located inside an open frame, the frame protects the sensing wires from damage while allowing a free flow of air over the wires. The exposed wires make up the hot junction. A cold junction is located behind insulating material in the sensor unit. Where there is a difference in temperature between the hot junction and the cold junction, a current is created. When sufficient current is being generated, a sensitive relay in a relay box closes, activating a slave relay and causing the alarm to activate.

19. A thermal switch system works at a specific temperature whereas the thermocouple system depends on a rate of temperature rise.
20. A test switch is used.
21. False fire warnings, caused by a short.
22. The small tubing is held in rubber or soft plastic grommets.
23. CO2 and Halogenated Hydrocarbons.
24. Nitrogen
25. 300-psi
26. From the manufacturer's date stamp on the face of the cartridge.
27. A pressure gauge or a "blowout" disk (red).
28. It indicates a normal system discharge.
29. The conventional system and the high-rate-of-discharge system (HRD system).
30. Dry-chemical type, a dry-gas type (CO_2), or a Halon 1301 type.